# A Good English Manual

# A Good English Manual

• A • •

# GOOD ENGLISH MANUAL

- Robert-Louis Abrahamson •
- Deborah Griggs •
- Maria Newkirk •
- Karen Olsen •
- Catherine Quinn •
- Patrick Quinn •

The University of Maryland, European Division

**Harper & Row, Publishers**

London

Cambridge  San Francisco
Mexico City      São Paulo
New York      Singapore
Philadelphia      Sydney

Series Editor: Dr Martha S. Shull, University of Maryland,
                European Division.

Designer: Geri Davis, Quadrata Inc.

Project Editor: Byron O. Bush.

First published 1988

Harper & Row Ltd
Middlesex House
34–42 Cleveland Street
LONDON
W1P 5FB

Library of Congress Cataloging-in-Publication Data
Good English Models.
    (The University of Maryland series on good
English writing)
    1. English language—Rhetoric.—Handbooks, manuals,
etc.  2. English language—Grammar—1950–    —Hand-
books, manuals, etc.   I. Abrahamson, Robert-Louis,
1949–   .  II. Series.
PE1408.G576   1988   808'.042   87–37341
ISBN 0-06-317502-9

British Library Cataloguing in Publication Data
A Good English manual.
    1. English language. Grammar
    I. Abrahamson, Robert-Louis
    428.2

    ISBN 0-06-317502-9

Typeset by Rowland Phototypesetting Limited, Bury St Edmunds, Suffolk.
Printed and bound by Richard Clay Limited, Chichester.

# ACKNOWLEDGMENTS

On behalf of the authors, I want to acknowledge and to applaud The University of Maryland, University College English faculty whose commitment to teaching adult learners has made this book possible.

I also would like to express appreciation and gratitude to all the instructors who field tested the texts, read and reread the drafts, and gave advice, suggestions, and encouragement: Carl Buchner, Denise Cali, Emily Chalmers, Douglas Cook, Thomas Crain, Jack Daugherty, Aimee Doyle, Maxine Feifer, Frank Funicello, Alison Goeller, Howard Hastings, Steven Kaplan, Lillian Klein, Tobe Levin, Kenneth Lewandoski, Judith Mossinger, Janet O'Bryant, James Pinnells, Richard Schumaker, Jayne Traendly, Mary Jo Van Ingen, and Nancy Wright.

Many thanks also go to Theresa Bowley, Judith Moses, and Denise Sokolowski who typed, retyped, proofread, and then did it all again; without you, the text might never have been put together properly. Thanks, too, to spouses and friends who listened and who encouraged us to keep on writing and rewriting.

I also take this opportunity to thank my fellow authors of *Good English Models*: Barbara Mayo-Wells, Jeanne McNett, and Robert Speckhard for their heartwarming encouragement and support of the entire project.

Lastly, I would like to express my gratitude to the students whose suggestions, assistance, essays, and paragraphs were infinitely helpful and for whom this project is intended.

Martha S. Shull
Series Editor

# CONTENTS

CONTENTS

CONTENTS

I can almost hear you say, "What, *another grammar*? Why would anyone go to all the trouble to write *another grammar*?" *A Good English Manual* was, however, written expressly for the adult student. In deciding to return to, to continue, or to begin a college education, the adult student often finds that he or she has forgotten many of the niceties of the English language as well as some of the essentials. This student needs a readable, practical short guide like this one to review English grammar and sentence skills.

*A Good English Manual* was also designed for use in an intensive, but relatively short college course in basic writing skills much like the term in the many divisions of University College, The University of Maryland. The European Division, the Asian Division, and the statewide programs of University College, The University of Maryland offer beginning composition classes that in eight weeks expect the returning adult student to learn to review the necessary grammar, spelling, and punctuation to write good sentences, complete paragraphs, and acceptable essays on the college level. *A Good English Manual* was written with just such adult students as these in mind who are learning under just such time constraints as these.

*A Good English Manual* was written not to replace an English grammar handbook, for one is essential for expository writing or in advanced writing courses. Like an up-to-date dictionary and a thesaurus, a good handbook is always a valuable addition to a writer's shelf of books. This little guide is, however, the outcome of the experience gleaned from teaching hundreds of beginning classes for adult students and was conceived to serve as a handy, short reference and review guide.

Martha S. Shull
Series Editor

# ONE

# Parts of Speech

## Introduction to the Sentence •

In school (and we're aware that it may have been a while), you might remember learning the definition of a **sentence** as *a complete idea*. Put that definition to the test by examining the word

"Ouch!"

Does the word express a complete thought? Well, it communicates slight discomfort, pain, or even agony, so the *idea* is definitely there. Is it, then, a sentence?

Any curious reader would probably appreciate some specific information about the "Ouch!" Who or what, for example, is the cause of the "Ouch"? What is the perpetrator of the crime doing to produce the "Ouch"? The answer to these questions may be found in the following group of words:

That dog bit me.

CHAPTER ONE

Although a simple idea may be expressed by only one word, such as "Ouch," a group of words is necessary if a *complete idea* is to be communicated. Such a group of words must tell who or what is performing the action—the **subject** in grammatical terms; the word group must also inform the reader exactly what the subject is doing, or in other words what the action is—the **predicate** in grammar. Thus, our group of words now breaks down into two distinct parts:

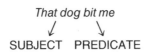

If a word group contains these three elements—

1. A complete idea
2. A subject (who or what is doing the action)
3. A predicate (what that subject is doing)

—then it will generally qualify as a **sentence**, known also for the time being as a **main clause**.

Of course, a little experience with sentence analysis will show the reader that there is an exception to many a rule, for sometimes even the most impressive main clause fails to make sense when read out of context. For example, the sentence "The problem with this technique is its facile symbolism" means nothing until it is placed within a paragraph of related sentences:

> Black and white photography in a color film is often employed for symbolic purposes. Some directors alternate whole episodes in black and white with entire sequences in color. The problem with this technique is its facile symbolism. The bleached black and white sequences are too jolting, too obviously "Symbolic" in the most corny sense.[1]

Structurally, sentences should be able to stand alone, but our full understanding of a sentence's meaning often depends upon the words surrounding it.

## • Finding the Essential Parts of a Sentence

In many cases, subjects and predicates fail to reveal themselves immediately because they may consist of more than one word each. For example, a

---

[1]Giannetti, Louis D. *Understanding Movies.* 2nd ed. Englewood Cliffs, NJ: Prentice Hall, 1976, p. 28.

slightly more interesting sentence on the theme of savage dogs than the simple "Dog bites" could read as follows:

> That lousy, good-for-nothing, flea-bitten mongrel dog next door bites me viciously every morning on my way to work.

Who or what is doing the action?

> (That lousy, good-for-nothing, flea-bitten mongrel dog next door) = COMPLETE SUBJECT

What is the subject doing? What is the action itself?

> (bites me viciously every morning on my way to work.) = COMPLETE PREDICATE

Here, the old cliché "can't see the forest for the trees" is valid because the extra bits and pieces in the sentence tend to clutter up our perception of exactly which word acts as the subject and which word makes a statement about that subject. In order to simplify matters—to seek out the **simple subject** and the **simple predicate**—imagine that you must write a telegram and that you can afford to pay for only two words. Now isolate the two most important elements of the main clause:

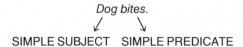

Other details in this sentence (or main clause) are present simply to add interest and precision to the idea.

Another example:

> After driving their Chevy to the levee where the river was dry, the good old *boys* slowly *lifted* Vera out of the oozing mud.

To isolate the simple subject and predicate, ask yourself exactly *who did what?*

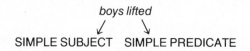

# The Simple Subject: Nouns & Pronouns •

Two parts of speech are able to function as the simple subject of a sentence: **nouns** (or groups of words acting as nouns) or **pronouns**.

## • Nouns

A noun is a naming word whose function is to identify anything and anybody. Often preceded by **the**, **a**, or **an**, a noun can name:

> OBJECTS: table, computer, carburetor, sock, map, ashtray, nose
> BEINGS: teacher, reptile, moose, stripper, clown, president
> PLACES: country, kitchen, campus, forest, bathroom, world
> ABSTRACT CONCEPTS: strife, toil, grief, grammar, justice, darkness

Basically, if it names, it's a noun.

The type of noun that labels words such as those above, without specifying exactly *which ones* (i.e., city, but not *which* city; moose, but not *which* moose) are **common nouns**.

The names of *specific* objects, persons, places, and ideas are capitalized for easy recognition and are **proper nouns**.

| COMMON | PROPER |
|--------|--------|
| dog | Bowser |
| boy | George |
| pen | Bic |
| city | Erie, PA |
| moose | Bullwinkle |
| cake | Twinkie |
| spaceship | U.S.S. Enterprise |

### Collective Nouns

Another noun species, collective nouns "collect" a number of like creatures or objects together to form a singular noun that represents the group:

> herd (cows)     school (dolphins)     tribe (pygmies)
> gaggle (geese)     team (tennis players)     class (students)

## • Pronouns

Students of Latin will immediately recognize the prefix of the word **pronoun** to mean "for." A pronoun does exactly what its name suggests; it

PARTS OF SPEECH

stands in *for* a noun, when noun usage becomes repetitious or clumsy. The noun to which a pronoun refers is its **antecedent**.

*The skunk* is my favorite beast.
↓
*It* radiates an exquisite fragrance.
("skunk" = antecedent of pronoun "it")

Grammarians bring pronouns to life by labelling them "persons." These "persons" are listed in a special order according to rank and number, and learning how the list works can help you not only in understanding verb forms, but also in studying a foreign language.

|  | SINGULAR | PLURAL |
|---|---|---|
| 1st PERSON | I | we |
| 2nd PERSON | you (refers to just one) | you (refers to two or more) |
| 3rd PERSON | he | |
| | she | they |
| | it | |

The personal pronouns listed above are labelled **subject pronouns** since their full-time job is to serve as the subject of a sentence. The grammatical phenomenon that distinguishes a subject pronoun from any other sort of pronoun—**case**—also determines the appearance of other pronouns according to their function in a sentence; for example, if a pronoun acts as the subject of a sentence, its case is the **subjective** case (*I, he, she*, etc.), but if a pronoun's job is to serve as a direct object (see p. 13) or as the object of a preposition (see p. 28), its case is **objective** (*me, him, her*, etc.). Other pronouns listed here are **possessive** and **reflexive**.

| | SUBJECTIVE* | OBJECTIVE* | REFLEXIVE | POSSESSIVE |
|---|---|---|---|---|
| 1 | I | me | myself | mine |
| 2 | you | you | yourself | yours |
| 3 | he | him | himself | his |
| | she | her | herself | hers |
| | it | it | itself | its |
| 1 | we | us | ourselves | ours |
| 2 | you | you | yourselves | yours |
| 3 | they | them | themselves | theirs |

*In the study of foreign languages, subjective and objective cases are often referred to as **nominative** and **accusative** respectively.

ONLY NOUNS AND PRONOUNS (TOGETHER WITH GROUPS OF WORDS ACTING AS NOUNS) MAY ACT AS THE SUBJECTS OF SENTENCES.

CHAPTER ONE

# The Simple Predicate: Verbs •

The most important element in the predicate of a main clause is the **verb**. In school, you probably learned that a verb is an "action word" and, indeed, when students are asked to name verbs, they inevitably come up with *run, leap, fly, fall, dash, jump*. If these were the only verbs available, we should all have to live as quasi-superhumans; but fortunately for the less active among us, more sedate verbs exist such as *stroll, lumber, sit, recline, lie, sleep, doze*.

Verbs *are* action words, but students must bear in mind that certain verbs are less muscular than others. Verbs like *imagine, think, dream, ponder, wonder*, for example, denote actions of the mind. (And what, after all, is the brain but one big muscle?) Do not ignore these mind-action verbs, for they play a large part in the English language.

Juliet *contemplated* the hopelessness of her love for Ron

describes an action just as much as

Darth *zapped* the invader with his laser gun.

Verbs are much more complex than nouns. Much of our knowledge of verbs is instinctive, but in many cases verb patterns are mislearned in childhood and must be corrected in adulthood, long after the learning process has taken place. One of the problems with verbs is that they exhibit different characteristics (called "properties" by grammarians) depending on the way that they are used in a sentence. The following few paragraphs explain what is meant by verb properties such as **tense**, **mood**, and **voice**.

## • Tense

Tense is not only how a student feels before a grammar test, but it also denotes the time when a verb's action occurs. The verb form itself changes according to its tense. In a **regular** verb, tenses change according to a strict formula. As an example, consider the regular verb *to talk*. What looks like a verb *talk* preceded by the word *to* is called an **infinitive**. The infinitive *to talk* is the generic form of the verb from which the verb is **conjugated** or put through its paces—*I talk, she talks, we talked, he will talk*, etc.

PARTS OF SPEECH

INFINITIVE *TO TALK*

| PRESENT TENSE | PAST TENSE |
|---|---|

(Add **s** to the infinitive for the 3rd person singular)

(Add **-ed** to the infinitive for all persons)

| | | | | |
|---|---|---|---|---|
| 1 | I | talk | I | talk**ed** |
| 2 | you | talk | you | talk**ed** |
| 3 | he | talk**s*** | he | talk**ed** |
| | she | talk**s**** | she | talk**ed** |
| | it | talk**s** | it | talk**ed** |
| 1 | we | talk | we | talk**ed** |
| 2 | you | talk | you | talk**ed** |
| 3 | they | talk | they | talk**ed** |

*Note a spelling modification in the case of certain verbs like *fly*—he, she, it flies/*catch*—he, she, it catches etc.

**The fact that an s is added to the third person singular form of the verb does not make it plural. Remember, these are verbs, not nouns. An often used formula goes like this: When the subject ends in s, add nothing to the verb; when the subject has no s ending, add s to the verb. Thus,

The cheese**s** stink
The cheese stink**s**
BUT . . .
Thoma**s** stink**s**!

## Irregular Verbs

Irregular verbs are "real originals." They follow no set pattern but their own and change their whole appearance when conjugated in the past tense. Not for them a regular **-ed** ending:

| INFINITIVE | PAST TENSE |
|---|---|
| to run | — I ran |
| to fly | — we flew |
| to speak | — she spoke |

The most troublesome of these irregular verbs, and therefore (according to Murphy's Law) the most used, is the verb *to be*:

CHAPTER ONE

| SUBJECT PRONOUN | PRESENT | PAST |
|---|---|---|
| I | am | was |
| you | are | were |
| he,she,it | is | was |
| we | are | were |
| you | are | were |
| they | are | were |

The verb *to be* becomes "user friendly" only when its conjugation is learned correctly.

## Auxiliary Verbs

Tenses other than the present and the simple past require the help of other verbs—**auxiliary verbs** (sometimes called **helping verbs**)—to assist the meaning of the main verb. The most common auxiliary verbs are *to be* and *to have*, and as many as three such verbs may be used to help one main verb. Note how many tenses may be formed with the use of auxiliary verbs:

| | |
|---|---|
| FUTURE: | I *will (shall)* go/I*will (shall)* be going |
| PRESENT PERFECT: | I *have* gone/I *have been* going |
| PAST PERFECT: | I *had* gone/I *had been* going |
| FUTURE PERFECT: | I *will (shall) have* gone/I *will (shall) have been* going |

## Modal Verbs

Modal verbs may be classed as auxiliaries because their function is also to help the main verb of the sentence. Rather than implying the time when an action occurs, however, modals indicate *ability* (I *can* fly), *permission* (You *may* leave the table), *obligation* (Soldiers *must* learn to obey orders), and *possibility* (That *might* be the answer).

The following list includes the most common modal verbs:

| | | | |
|---|---|---|---|
| can | may | must | should |
| could | might | ought | would |

## *To do* as a Helping Verb

*To do* is a fine action verb in its own right. It can, however, fulfil a part-time function as a helping verb when it is followed by a main verb with the following results:

| | |
|---|---|
| To express a question: | *Do* you dance? |
| To give emphasis: | She *does* move well. |
| To form the negative (with *not*): | No, I *did* not eat the last piece of pie. |

## Participles

With the exception of the future tense, all auxiliary verbs are followed by **participles**, of which each verb has two—a **present participle** (formed by adding *ing* to the infinitive) and a **past participle** (formed by adding *ed* to the infinitive; it looks just like the past tense).

| INFINITIVE | PRESENT PARTICIPLE | PAST PARTICIPLE |
|---|---|---|
| To help | help**ing** | help**ed** |
| To aid | aid**ing** | aid**ed** |
| To support | support**ing** | support**ed** |

Inevitably, irregular verbs come back to haunt us. Although (with no exceptions) they form their present participles regularly by adding 'ing' to the infinitive, their past participles have frustrated many a writer, and must often be re-learned by rote. Listed here are the top ten most commonly abused past participles. Notice that none of them add the regular **-ed** ending for past participles. (See p. 145 for a more exhaustive list of irregular verbs.)

| | | | |
|---|---|---|---|
| To run | — I have run | To drink | — I have drunk |
| To go | — I have gone | To eat | — I have eaten |
| To be | — I have been | To drive | — I have driven |
| To choose | — I have chosen | To see | — I have seen |
| To bring | — I have brought | To break | — I have broken |

The past participle and past tense of a verb, together with its infinitive form, are called collectively the **principal parts** of the verb. The principal parts of the verb **to eat**, for example, would be as follows:

| INFINITIVE | PAST TENSE | PAST PARTICIPLE |
|---|---|---|
| **to eat** | **ate** | **eaten** |

You can find the principal parts of irregular verbs in a dictionary to help you conjugate all tenses correctly.

## • Mood

Earlier, it was suggested that grammarians personify pronouns by treating them as "persons." Similarly, mention should be made of the fact that verbs, like humans, can be affected by **mood**. The mood of a verb, in fact, gives us a clue as to the disposition of the writer or speaker.

Ordinarily, when we make statements, impart information, or indicate what is happening, we write or speak in the **indicative** mood:

Boy, I *am* smart!
Joe *is staying* in the army.
Rover *sat* in the doghouse from noon until dusk.

If, on the other hand, we are feeling imperious and our aim is to make the reader or listener jump to attention and obey, we use the **imperative** mood to make commands:

Be smart!
Stay in the army!
Rover, sit!

Finally, the **subjunctive** mood, which is seldom used in colloquial English, continues to play a part in formal speech and writing. We find it in expressions beginning with *if* to express what might be, but isn't or in the statement of a wish or request. The subjunctive mood affects the verb *to be* in particular:

I wish I *were* clever.
If only he *were* in the army . . .
If Rover *were* allowed to sit on your lap, he'd be much happier.

Other verbs too can appear in the subjunctive:

I wish he *came* every day.
I wouldn't be surprised if it *rained* tomorrow.

## • Voice

**Voice** indicates whether the subject of a sentence is actively *performing* or passively *receiving* an action.

**Active voice** occurs where the subject of a sentence performs the action of a verb. **Passive voice**, which is formed by part of the verb *to be* plus a past participle, occurs where the subject of a sentence receives the action of a verb. Compare the following sentences to determine the different effects a writer may achieve by careful selection of voice. (See p. 89.)

PASSIVE: A Fender guitar *was borrowed* by Jeff so that the group could play at the next local dance.

ACTIVE: Jeff *borrowed* a Fender guitar so that the group could play at the next local dance.

PASSIVE: It *was reported* by the neighborhood Peeping Tom that the crime *was committed* by a little old lady wearing a Lone Ranger mask.

ACTIVE: The neighborhood Peeping Tom *reported* that a little old lady wearing a Lone Ranger mask *committed* the crime.

# More About Sentence Structure •

When studying a language as complex as English, we must learn to expect and accept its inherent eccentricities (irregular verbs for example) or give up altogether. One surprisingly benevolent aspect of English grammar, however, is that its main clauses may appear only in a limited number of forms or sentence patterns. Although English burdens its students with some eighty irregular past participles, it offers only five basic patterns of the simple sentence.

By learning the components of these sentence patterns, writers may improve their prose; they can learn to spot the repetition of any one pattern in their writing and thus vary their style for improvement. (See Chapter Four, p. 116.) With some knowledge of the five sentence patterns, they can also avoid committing gross grammatical errors—the sorts of mistakes that separate the literate from the illiterate.*

*The car ran real good.

## • Pattern 1: Subject/Verb (S/V)

Pattern 1 (S/V) sentences, which can be recognized by their **subject/verb** formula, may be very simple—

*Pigs fly*

—or as complicated as a writer pleases:

On a dark winter's eve, the whining *wind curled* around the old stone
   cottages of the hillside village.
*Spock sleeps* with his eyes open.
The *sound* of heavy metal *pounded* through the auditorium.

The basic components, however, remain the subject and the verb (or verbs, if auxiliaries are involved). The functions of other words or phrases in these main clauses are to describe the subject (*whining*—wind/*of heavy metal* —sound) or to modify the verb (*with his eyes open*—sleeps/*through the auditorium*—pounded).

### Compound Subjects and Verbs

You might remember from chemistry lessons at school that mixing two elements in a test tube generally results in either a big bang or a compound. In English, when writers combine two elements—two subjects, for example—and force them to share the same verb in one main clause, they create a **compound subject**:

*Jack and Jill* went up the Eiffel Tower

Conversely, when we force two verbs to share the same subject in a main clause, we create a compound verb:

Old King Cole *ate and drank* to excess.

# • Pattern 2: Subject/Verb/Direct Object (S/V/DO)

The subject of a sentence may sometimes impose the action it performs upon another noun or pronoun in the same main clause. Compare the following two sentences:

That cat scratches.

Subject = *cat*/Verb = *scratches*

That cat scratches *people.*

Subject = *cat*/Verb = *scratches*

But how does the word *people* fit in? *People* are the ones being scratched; they are on the other end of the scratching.
  Another example:

That cat claws *babies.*

| | |
|---|---|
| Who or what is doing the clawing? | *That cat* (subject) |
| What is that cat doing? | *claws* (verb) |
| Who or what is being clawed? | |
| Who or what is on the other end of the clawing? | *babies* |

The element that is on the other end of the action, the person or object being "verb-ed" (scratched, clawed, chewed, bitten, etc.) is called the **direct object**, for it is the part of the sentence which is directly affected by the action that the subject performs.

ONLY NOUNS AND PRONOUNS (TOGETHER WITH GROUPS OF WORDS ACTING AS NOUNS) MAY ACT AS DIRECT OBJECTS

Consider the following examples of pattern 2 (S/V/DO) sentences, and observe the function and position of the direct object in each case. Remember that only nouns and pronouns (or groups of words acting as nouns) may act as subjects or direct objects.

I really like *the guy* with the Mohican haircut.

(The guy = *the object* of my affection)

The child tossed *her cookies* overboard.

(Cookies = what are being tossed)

No sane person ever visits *Cleveland.*

(Cleveland = what is not being visited)

Tonight I ate *Rolaids* for dessert.

(Rolaids = what I ate for dessert)

## Pronouns as Objects

Note that pronouns change from the **subjective** case to the **objective** case as their function in the sentence changes from subject to object:

I saw *him* . . . *he* saw *me*.
*They* came to our door. We invited *them* in.

The forms change to ensure that the listener or reader understands exactly who or what the subject/object is (see **case** p. 5).

## Transitive and Intransitive Verbs

The type of verb that appears in pattern 2 (S/V/DO) sentences is able to *transfer* its action onto a direct object, and thus is called a **transitive** verb. In the next examples, the verbs *carry, presented, lays, raised,* and *include* are transitive because they take direct objects.

We *carry wood* each day from the forest to the house.
Mrs. Griswold *presented her daughter* to the Duchess.
The chicken *lays its eggs* all in one basket.
W. C. Fields *raised a few glasses* too many.
Fortunately, the most recent fifties revival *did* not *include a return* to the hula hoop.

A few select verbs, on the other hand, would not be caught dead in a S/V/DO sentence. These verbs—*intransitive* **verbs**—have no power to transfer their action onto a direct object and consequently are to be found only in S/V sentences:

The genie *disappeared* in a flash.*
I can't *cope* with all these long words.*
Every Sunday morning, we *lie* in bed until noon.*
The sun *rises* on another halcyon day.*

*The verbs here are followed by modifying phrases. (See prepositional phrases, p. 28.)

Many verbs are changeable because they are able to span both categories; they are able to do both jobs—to act transitively or intransitively—depending upon the context in which they are placed:

| TRANSITIVE | INTRANSITIVE |
|---|---|
| Seb runs *ten kilometers* every night. | He runs quickly and gracefully. |
| Last night I drove *my mother* crazy. | Tomorrow we are driving to L.A. |
| A good athlete can jump *a five-foot bar*. | Sue was jumping for joy. |

The distinction between transitive and intransitive verbs is perhaps best explained by the story of the three sons of the McVerb family:

The eldest son, Trevor McVerb, an excitable and energetic sort of youth, *enjoyed* action. In a typical day, he would *run* errands, *hit* tennis balls, *slam* doors, *study* grammar, *drink* beers, and *chase* women. In the evenings, Trevor *fixed* cars, *cleaned* his room, *milked* the cows on the McVerb farm, and *lectured* his lazy brother Ian.  } TRANSITIVE

Ian *was* a dreamer. He *felt* miserable when faced with any activity requiring effort. Instead, Ian would *rise* late in the morning, *stay* in his room all day, *lie* on the couch, and *think* about life. He *was* always too tired for anything physical and would *feel* unhappy if Trevor asked him to make supper or wash dishes. Ian would *slink* off and *rest* in his room.  } INTRANSITIVE

There *was* one more member of the McVerb family—Charlie—who had *inherited* a few of each of his elder brothers' characteristics. Charlie generally *liked* action, but he *was* a moody child. Depending on the nature of the task and his mood, Charlie would sometimes *play* tennis and *help* Trevor, or he would *slouch* off and *sulk* with Ian whose desire to remain inactive he well *understood*. Once Trevor and Charlie *were* out *running* a race and during the very last lap, Charlie simply *stopped* and *disappeared*. From time to time he would *want* action and excitement, and at other times he would *be* as lethargic as Ian; it just *depended* on the conditions around him.  } BOTH

## Lay and Lie/Raise and Rise

If we were to award prizes in grammar, we would no doubt select the following verbs as winners in their own special categories:

| | |
|---|---|
| Most Irregular: | to be |
| Most Active: | to run |
| Most Troublesome: | to lie/lay |
| | to rise/raise |

These last four verbs, though, are not quite so difficult as appearances would suggest. A writer must simply

1. learn their principal parts, and

2. be able to distinguish the transitive verbs from the intransitive:

| | PRINCIPAL PARTS | | | | MEANING |
|---|---|---|---|---|---|
| INTRANSITIVE: | *To lie:* | lie, | lay, | have lain | —to rest or to recline |
| TRANSITIVE: | *To lay:* | lay, | laid, | have laid | —to place or to put |
| INTRANSITIVE: | *To rise:* | rise, | rose, | have risen | —to get up or go up |
| TRANSITIVE: | *To raise:* | raise, | raised, | have raised | —to lift up or to help grow |

Notice that both transitive verbs follow the regular pattern (with a spelling modification in the case of *laid*) of adding **d/-ed** to the infinitive to form the past tense and the past participle. The two intransitive verbs are irregular.

| TRANSITIVE | INTRANSITIVE |
|---|---|
| The hens *lay* eggs every day. | Fred *lies* in the bath for relaxation. |
| The workers *laid* floor tiles in less than one day. | John and Yoko *lay* in bed for over a week. |
| The cowboys have *laid* a trap for the cattle rustlers. | Sue has *lain* in the sun all day; now she has sunstroke. |
| Sally raises daisies in her garden; I *raise* cane. | "I hope I can *rise* to the occasion," said the bun to the oven. |
| I *raised* the blinds when the day finally dawned. | When Willy finished his last song, all of Nashville *rose* and cheered. |
| Roger Clemens has *raised* his salary potential by winning the Cy Young Award. | When the exam was over, I felt as if I had *risen* from the dead. |

CHAPTER ONE

# • Pattern 3: Subject/Verb/Direct Object/Object Complement (S/V/DO/OC)

Sentence pattern 3 (S/V/DO/OC), although not nearly as frequently used as the previous two, still deserves a mention. It follows pattern 2 (S/V/DO) closely but adds to the end of the pattern 2 main clause another dimension—a noun or adjective whose function is to describe or refer to the direct object:

The jury judged *Smith innocent.*

The new dimension that refers to, describes, or complements the direct object is called, logically enough, the **object complement**. Furthermore, this sentence pattern is often voted "Everybody's Favorite" simply because of the limited number of verbs that it employs, among which are *proclaim, believe, consider, judge, make, call, name,* and *appoint.*

| PATTERN 2 | PATTERN 3 |
|---|---|
| Schlitz made *Milwaukee.* | Schlitz made *Milwaukee famous.* |
| The press called *Elvis.* | The press called *Elvis a has-been.* |
| We have named *our parrot.* | We have named *our parrot Butch.* |

**NOTE:** **Complements** are parts of speech that do exactly as their name suggests; they complement or complete the sense of the word to which they refer. **Object complements** modify direct objects in pattern 3 (S/V/DO/OC) sentences.

# • Pattern 4: Subject/Verb/Indirect Object/Direct Object (S/V/IO/DO)

In the fourth pattern of the simple sentence, we are introduced to yet another element of language that tells the reader exactly *for whom* or *to whom* an action is being done. Compare the following sentences:

   **a.** Everybody called Sam a weirdo.

   **b.** Bogie called Bacall a taxi.

In sentence (a), the last element—*weirdo*—refers directly to Sam, the direct object; since its job is to modify the direct object, *weirdo* is an **object complement**, and the sentence falls neatly into pattern 3 (S/V/DO/OC). In sentence (b), though, it is highly unlikely that Bogie chose to insult Bacall by calling her *Taxi!* In fact, the word *taxi* has no direct relation to Bacall. Instead, we must presume that Bogie is calling a taxi *for* Bacall—that Bacall is the person *for whom* the action is being done.

Similarly, when a writer merges the following main clauses, we can determine *to* whom the action is being done:

We sold a raffle ticket.
We sold our grandmother. } We sold our grandmother a raffle ticket.

The raffle ticket is what is being sold (**direct object**); our grandmother is the person *to* whom the ticket is being sold.

The name of the element that tells a reader *for whom* or *to whom* an action is performed is the **indirect object**. Three important points to remember about the indirect object are as follows:

1. Only a noun or a pronoun may function as the indirect object of a sentence.

2. Although the job of the indirect object is to dictate *to whom* or *for whom* an action is performed, the words *to* or *for* are never actually written; instead, *to* or *for* might be said to float invisibly in front of the indirect object; they are understood rather than seen.

3. The indirect object will always be positioned in *front of* the direct object of a main clause; there are no exceptions to this rule.

I shot some grouse.
I shot my nephew. } I shot my nephew some grouse for his birthday.

Mr. Smith baked a cake.
Mr. Smith baked his wife. } Mr. Smith baked his wife a cake.

ONLY NOUNS OR PRONOUNS (TOGETHER WITH GROUPS OF WORDS ACTING AS NOUNS) MAY FUNCTION AS SUBJECTS, DIRECT OBJECTS, OR INDIRECT OBJECTS OF SENTENCES

## • Pattern 5: Subject/Linking Verb/Subject Complement (S/LV/SC)

The fifth pattern of the simple sentence generally gives itself away by the special type of verb it uses: the **linking verb**. As its name suggests, the linking verb links or bridges the gap between the subject of a main clause and a word* that describes, identifies, or refers to the subject—the **subject complement**.

*A predicate noun, pronoun, or adjective. See p. 21.

| | |
|---|---|
| *Joe* seemed *concerned* about his appearance. | (*Concerned* describes Joe) |
| *The Cubs* are *Number One!* | (*Number one* refers to the Cubs) |
| *An expensive car* is *a waste of money.* | (*Waste* modifies expensive car) |
| *Washington* became *president* in 1789 | (*President* identifies George Washington) |

Linking verbs are easy to cope with for two reasons:

First, there exist only a limited number of genuine linking verbs—*to be* (when it functions as the main verb), *to seem, to appear,* and *to become.* Other verbs are capable of functioning as linking verbs—*to taste, to feel, to smell, to look, to sound, to act*—but be aware that the latter group of verbs may also make appearances in other sentence patterns.

Second, since the purpose of linking verbs is merely to bridge the gap between **subject** and **subject complement**, they may be replaced at any time by either a simple *equals sign* (=) or a part of the verb *to be*:

| PATTERN 2 (S/V/DO) | PATTERN 5 (S/LV/SC) |
|---|---|
| Kitty tasted the lemon. | The lemon *tasted* bitter. (The lemon = (or) *was* bitter) |
| Martie felt the softness of the fabric with the palms of her hands. | The fabric *felt* soft and smooth. (The fabric = (or) *was* soft and smooth) |

By logical reasoning and careful analysis, you should always be able to tell whether a verb is acting **transitively** (i.e. whether it takes a direct object) or whether it is **linking** the subject to a word modifying or identifying the subject—the **subject complement**.

**Subject complements** modify subjects in pattern 5 (S/LV/SC) sentences. Only nouns, pronouns, and adjectives may act as subject complements.

## The Passive Voice & Sentence Pattern 5

Pattern 5 (S/LV/SC) sentences and main clauses containing a verb in the passive voice (see p. 10) are easily confused because of their one common denominator: the verb *to be.*

*To be* is, without doubt, the most frequently used linking verb when it acts as the main verb in a sentence:

The matador *was* brave.

*To be* can also act as a helping verb in the passive voice construction when it is followed by a past participle:

The bull *was taunted* by the matador.

PARTS OF SPEECH

Learn to distinguish one usage from the other.

In a passive voice construction, the subject of the sentence is the person or thing *receiving* the action of the verb rather than *performing* it. A part of the verb *to be* helps the past participle of the main verb.

In pattern 5 (S/LV/SC) sentences, on the other hand, the subject of the sentence is simply followed by *to be* (or another linking verb) whose function is to bridge the gap between subject and subject complement. No action transpires.

| PATTERN 5 | PASSIVE |
|---|---|
| This candidate *is* best qualified. | This candidate *is being considered* by the panel. |
| Our antenna *has been* faulty. | Our antenna *has been repaired.* |

# • Variations on a Theme

Once the process of identifying the subjects, objects, and complements of main clauses is fully understood, simple sentence analysis should follow easily. Be wary, though, of several variations on the five sentence patterns, for these will throw a wrench into the works of your sentence analysis. Always approach the main clause cautiously when you recognize any one of the following verb constructions:

## 1. The Passive Voice

This voice grabs the action of a sentence away from the one *performing* and instead concentrates on the one *receiving*. In passive voice constructions, the grammatical subject is not the one doing the action (see also p. 10):

I was given a box of pastel pink writing paper by my aunt for Christmas.

## 2. The Interrogative

The most frequently used formula for creating a question in English—the Interrogative form—simply inverts the subject and the verb. This, in turn, upsets the sentence pattern:

It is sunny today. *Is it* sunny today?
Onions are necessary to make good soup. *Are onions* necessary to make good soup?

## 3. The Imperative

Be assertive! Give a few commands. Drop the subject and use the Imperative (see also p. 10):

Go ahead . . . make my day!
Keep milk rotated in your refrigerator.

### 4. The Expletive

Expletives—words like *there* and *it*—simply upset the word order of a sentence by pushing the subject into third place after the verb. Really an excuse for avoiding the issue, expletives help a writer put off the inevitable until later and can result in sentences that are at least one word longer than necessary:

*There* is an elephant in the refrigerator.　　*An elephant* is in the refrigerator.

*It* is always hot in February in Tasmania.　　*February* is always hot in Tasmania.

# Modifiers •

If the study of grammar involved nothing more than learning the components of the five sentence patterns—the skeleton of the English language—then perhaps English would soar ahead of computer science and business studies as the most popular college major. This, however, is not to be; if the English language had only five possible variations, think how imprecise and uninteresting the process of written communication would be.

Consider that staple of the American diet: the hamburger. Now ask yourself which is more appetizing: a plain burger, or a Big Mac?

On its own, a plain hamburger is a complete meal since it is quite substantial in its content. For the majority of burger connoisseurs, however, the plain burger is also dull, unappetizing, and unattractive. A Big Mac, on the other hand, offers a variety of flavors; it is zesty and colorful, and its extra ingredients also supply additional nutrients to the plain burger. The Big Mac is bigger and, some would say, better.

In grammatical terms, subjects, verbs, objects, and complements form the basic necessities of the sentence, but alone they do not suffice to make language appetizing, interesting, and precise. A writer has the choice, however, of supplementing the main clause with other ingredients for extra flavor and substance. These supplements—we could call them grammatical relish—are known as modifiers.

## One Word Modifiers: Adjectives and Adverbs

## • Adjectives

An **adjective** modifies nouns (and thereby pronouns). In performing this task, an adjective can add detail to persons, places, objects, or ideas and thus make them interesting and specific.

Many adjectives are instantly recognizable, for they describe or modify the nouns and pronouns next to which they stand:

| | |
|---|---|
| *sarcastic* remark | Do you call that joke *funny*? |
| *black* cat | |
| *blithering* idiot | We proclaimed Joan *innocent*. |
| *silly* me | |

## Predicate Adjectives

Although the function of adjectives is to modify or limit nouns and pronouns, in pattern 5 sentences (S/LV/SC) a linking verb will sometimes separate them from the noun or pronoun they modify:

Richard Taft was *overweight*.
Bobby Jo looked *petrified*.
The diet soda tasted *bitter*.
Often, a high school education is *inadequate* to prepare a person for college.

These adjectives that modify the subject but get stuck in the predicate of a sentence are known as **predicate adjectives**.

## Nouns Acting as Adjectives

The flexibility of the English language allows us to take nouns and transform them into adjectives as in the following examples:

| | |
|---|---|
| *party* animal | *college* class |
| *porcelain* bowl | *Playboy* magazine |
| *hospital* ward | *history* teacher |

As a general rule, though, try to avoid using nouns as adjectives because the results will often be too colloquial and imprecise for formal writing (a *fun* class) or will ring of bureaucratic jargon (*command service* interface). (See p. 93.)

## Limiting Adjectives

Most adjectives are easily recognizable because of their powers of description—*small, fat, beige, beautiful, pure, happy*—but certain words qualify as adjectives more because they can **limit** nouns rather than **describe** them. These adjectives can be categorized in groups for the sake of simplicity:

CHAPTER ONE

## POSSESSIVE ADJECTIVES

| | |
|---|---|
| my | *my* camera |
| your (singular) | *your* campaign speech |
| his, her, its* | *her* elephant |
| our | *our* hats |
| your (plural) | *your* place |
| their | *their* job |

## DEMONSTRATIVE ADJECTIVES

| | |
|---|---|
| this, these | *this* old man, *these* days |
| that, those | *that* book, *those* children |

## RELATIVE ADJECTIVES

| | |
|---|---|
| which | The waiter asked *which wine* I preferred. |
| whose | That's the guy *whose car* I hit. |

## INTERROGATIVE ADJECTIVES

| | |
|---|---|
| which? | *Which book* were you required to read? |
| what? | *What sort* of reptile would you like? |
| whose? | *Whose car* did I just hit? |

## INDEFINITE ADJECTIVES

| | |
|---|---|
| each | *each* twin |
| another | *another* day |
| either | *either* color |
| neither | *neither* place |
| some | *some* cookies |

Note that when the noun is dropped from each of these phrases, the function of the solitary adjective is no longer to modify (for there is no noun to modify) but to stand in for the noun. In such cases, the adjectives become **pronouns**. Some change their forms slightly in order to fulfil their new task; others remain the same:

| | ADJECTIVE | PRONOUN |
|---|---|---|
| POSSESSIVE | That's *my* car. | That's *mine*. |
| | That's *your* poodle. | That's *yours*. |
| | That's *her* shirt. | That's *hers*. |
| | That's *his* text. | That's *his*. |
| | That's *our* house. | That's *ours*. |
| | That's *their* job. | That's *theirs*. |

PARTS OF SPEECH

|  | ADJECTIVE | PRONOUN |
|---|---|---|
| DEMONSTRATIVE | Is *that book* yours?<br>*This subject* bores me. | Is *that* yours?<br>*This* bores me. |
| RELATIVE/<br>INTERROGATIVE | The teacher asked *which class* we liked best.<br>*Whose dog* is this? | She asked *which* we liked best.<br>*Whose* is this? |
| INDEFINITE | There goes *another jet.*<br>*Each child* takes its own lunch.<br>*Either choice* would work. | There goes *another.*<br>*Each* takes its own.<br>*Either* would work. |

*Possessive pronouns *never* show possession by adding an apostrophe; they don't need to, for after all they are already possessive. Be especially careful to distinguish between the possessive pronoun *its* and the subject/verb contraction *it's* where the apostrophe stands in for the missing **i** of the verb *is.* (See also, Chapter Two, p. 56.)

### Definite and Indefinite Articles

Although they do not describe as such, the **definite article** *the* and the **indefinite articles** *a* and *an* qualify as adjectives because they are able to limit nouns. *The moose* refers to a specific moose (a **definite** moose), whereas the identity of just *a moose* is not known (it is **indefinite**). (See also Chapter Three, p. 97.)

## • Adverbs

Unlike adjectives, which modify nouns and pronouns, adverbs modify a wide variety of words.

First, adverbs are best known for the interest that they add to **verbs**:

Palmer *cautiously* putted the ball.
Joan Collins gestured *wildly* but certainly not *dramatically*.
Peeping Tom crept *sneakily* up to the open window.

Second, adverbs can also modify **adjectives**:

She wore an *extremely* expensive outfit; her shoes were made of *incredibly* fine leather, and her dress was one of *impeccably* good taste. Clothed in all of this finery, her dirty fingernails were *scarcely* noticeable.

CHAPTER ONE

Third, adverbs can modify other **adverbs**:

Are you hungry? You ate your dinner *awfully* quickly.
Jane's sprained ankle forced her to walk *extremely* awkwardly.

ADVERBS CAN MODIFY VERBS, ADJECTIVES, AND OTHER
ADVERBS

## "Irregular" Adverbs

Adverbs are normally recognizable by their **-ly** ending, but there are certain adverbs that refuse to conform to this standard; Murphy's Law again dictates that the following **irregular** adverbs be the most frequently used:

*very—almost—so—quite—rather—too—somewhat*

Our teacher was always *very* serious.
The basketball coach is *almost* seven feet tall.

In fact, some adverbs—such as *slow, fast, just, early*, and *hard*—determine to confuse students by disguising themselves as adjectives. A quick analysis of the sentence will usually suffice to determine how the word is functioning.

| ADJECTIVE | ADVERB |
|---|---|
| The *early* bird gets the worm. | We got up *early* this morning. |
| That was a *hard* course. | Our teacher made us work *hard*. |

**NOTE:** The words *not* and *never* are also adverbs.

## Tips on Spotting Adverbs

First, the position of an adverb in a sentence is usually flexible. Where adjectives are generally static, adverbs may move around a clause.

**a.** When visiting teams come to town, they *usually* stay at the Hilton.

**b.** *Usually* when visiting teams come to town, they stay at the Hilton.

Second, adverbs often answer the following questions:

**How?** (expressions of manner)
Seb ran the race *quite* quickly. (How quickly? *Quite quickly*.)

**When?** (expressions of time)
I fell on my face *yesterday*.    (When did I fall? *Yesterday*.)

**Where?** (expressions of location)
Let's go *home* now.   (Where shall we go? *Home.*)

**How often?** (expressions of frequency)
She rides her bike to work *daily*.   (How often does she ride? *Daily.*)

**NOTE:** The adjective and adverb pairs *good/well* and *real/really* are commonly misused:

WRONG:   David swims good.
RIGHT:   David is a *good* swimmer. He swims *well*.
              (Adjective = *good*/Adverb = *well*)
WRONG:   The car ran real slow.
RIGHT:   The car was a *real* lemon. It ran *really* slowly.
              (Adjective = *real*/Adverbs = *really* & *slowly*)

# • Comparative and Superlative Forms

The adjectives and adverbs dealt with thus far are the **positive** forms, which are used to describe or modify one item only.

That was a *funny* movie.

## The Comparative

When we compare one item to another, we must change the modifier to its **comparative** form either by adding the suffix **-er** (if the word is of one or two syllables) or by adding the adverbs *more* or *less* to the positive forms of longer words.

| POSITIVE | | COMPARATIVE |
|---|---|---|
| slow | (adj) | slow*er* |
| slowly | (adv) | slowl*ier* (note spelling change) |
| white | (adj) | whit*er* |
| beautifully | (adv) | *more* beautifully |
| general | (adj) | *less* general |

There are, of course, certain exceptions to the syllable rule, such as

| sure | (adj) | *more* sure (never "surer") |
|---|---|---|
| certain | (adj) | *more* certain (never "certainer") |

CHAPTER ONE

## TWO WORDS OF CAUTION

1. Never use the two comparative techniques (-**er** & *more*) together, such as in: "My dad is more bigger than your dad!"

2. Use the comparative form of the adjective or adverb only when you are comparing two items (not three or more):

> Although Paul is the *smaller* of the two Whitworth children, he is *stronger* than his sister Kate.

## The Superlative

In order to show the greatest degree of quantity or quality in an adjective or adverb, we must change the positive form of the modifier to its **superlative** state either by adding the suffix -**est** (if the word is of one or two syllables) or by adding the adverbs *most* or *least* to the positive forms of longer words.

| POSITIVE | COMPARATIVE | SUPERLATIVE |
|----------|-------------|-------------|
| slow | slower | slow*est* |
| beautiful | more beautiful | *most* beautiful |
| sure | more sure | *most* sure |
| special | more special | *most* special |

Use the superlative to indicate the maximum degree among three or more items:

> Joseph was the *smallest* of the quintuplets; Patrick was the *liveliest*, Mary the *kindest*, and Rhia the *funniest*; Sebastian was the *most sensitive* of the five.

Watch out for a few irregular comparative and superlative forms:

| (adj) | good | better | best |
|-------|------|--------|------|
| (adv) | well | better | best |
| (adj) | bad | worse | worst |
| (adv) | badly | worse | worst |
| (adj/adv) | far | farther/further | farthest/furthest |
| (adj) | many | more | most |
| (adj/adv) | much | more | most |
| (adj/adv) | little* | less* | least* |

*Use *little, less,* and *least* with singular nouns; use *few, fewer,* and *fewest* with plural nouns. (See also p. 134.)

PARTS OF SPEECH

As a child, Clive had *less* money and *fewer* opportunities than his friends, but despite these obstacles, he used his brawn and a Mohican haircut to make his fortune as a pro-wrestler.

ADJECTIVES MODIFY NOUNS AND PRONOUNS
ADVERBS MODIFY VERBS, ADJECTIVES, AND OTHER ADVERBS

# Modifying Phrases

Modifying phrases are groups of words that are able to describe nouns, verbs, adjectives, and adverbs just as effectively as one-word modifiers. Modifying phrases, in fact, could be seen as "stretched-out" adjectives and adverbs themselves.

**NOTE:** A phrase is simply a group of words that belong together; it has neither subject nor predicate:

under the spreading chestnut tree
before turning into a frog
on a daily basis

# • Expressions of Time

When a group of words in a sentence limits the time at which an action occurs—when it tells *when*—the chances are that it is an **adverb phrase**.

ADVERB PHRASE

*Last summer*, we camped by Lake Ontario.
We were married *two years ago*.

Learn to distinguish between expressions of time that act as adverbs (stating *when*) and those phrases that function as integral parts of the sentence structure (an expression of time acting as the subject, for example).

SUBJECT

*Last summer* was glorious.
*These past two years* have been the best of times and the worst of times.

# • Prepositional Phrases

The standard school definition of the way in which prepositions function is that they signify anything a squirrel can do with a tree. Fair enough: a squirrel can go *up* a tree, *down* a tree, *around* it, *under* it, *away from* it, *towards* it, *behind* it, *inside* it (if the tree is hollow) and even *through* it (if the squirrel has sharp incisors and lots of staying power); if two trees are available, the squirrel may go *between* them.

Squirrels aside, though, there are a number of valid prepositions that fail to fit our high school definition; below is a list of the most commonly used prepositions—words that generally indicate location, but that always help relate one thing to another.

| about | before | despite | near | throughout | with |
| above | behind | down | next to | to | within |
| across | below | during | of | toward | without |
| after | beneath | except | off | towards | |
| against | beside | for | on | under | |
| along | besides | from | onto | underneath | |
| among | between | inside | out of | until | |
| around | beyond | in | over | unto | |
| as | by | into | past | up | |
| at | concerning | like | through | upon | |

Prepositions cannot function alone; their very name suggests that they are "pre-positioned" with, or placed before, another word: a noun or a pronoun. Thus, the group of words that comprises a preposition together with its noun or pronoun (its object) is called a **prepositional phrase**.

No matter where prepositional phrases fall in a sentence, they always have a job to do—that of modifying other elements in the sentence. (See also connecting words, p. 35.)

## Adjective Prepositional Phrases

As their name suggests, adjective prepositional phrases act as stretched-out modifiers of nouns and pronouns.

The house *of the rising sun*

A man *about town*

The shade *under the greenwood tree*

**Note:** Adjectives sometimes follow the words they modify. Prepositional phrases acting as adjectives always follow the words they modify.

PARTS OF SPEECH

### Adverb Prepositional Phrases

These extended adverbs can modify verbs, adjectives, and other adverbs. Like adverbs, they can also answer the questions *how? when? where? how often?* and *why?*

> We left *after the party*. (when?)
> He died *for his country*. (why?)
> They went *to the lighthouse*.* (where?)

*Don't confuse prepositional phrases beginning with *to* with infinitives. An infinitive contains a verb form, whereas the preposition *to* is always followed by a noun or a pronoun.

> INFINITIVES: to run, to skip, to eat, to bellow
> PREPOSITIONAL PHRASES: to the store, to bed, to school, to me

### Adverbs that Masquerade as Prepositions

The function of a preposition is to link its object (a noun or pronoun) to another word in the sentence. Thus, a preposition is only a preposition if it is followed by a noun or pronoun acting as its object. Words that resemble prepositions but have no objects are simply adverbs whose job is to modify, but not to connect. Adverbs that masquerade as prepositions are not followed by nouns.

| ADVERB | PREPOSITION |
| --- | --- |
| Do you want to come *along*? | We walked *along the wooded lane*. |
| Roll *over*, Beethoven! | That fellow is really *over the hill*. |

ONLY NOUNS AND PRONOUNS MAY ACT AS THE OBJECTS OF
PREPOSITIONS

## • Verbal Phrases

When is a verb *not* a verb? When it's a **verbal**.

A word may be identified as a verb if it has a subject and if it makes a statement about that subject. Some verbs, as we have already discovered, need more than one word to express their tense, mood, or voice; in such cases we enlist the help of an auxiliary or two together with the main verb of the clause which transforms itself into a participle—

> I *should have broken* his neck!
> We *were* even *dancing* on the ceiling.

—or into an infinitive:

But it *was* not *to be.*

*Without* their auxiliaries, participles and infinitives lose their verb power, for they are no longer able to make a statement:

I . . . *broken*
We . . . *dancing*
It . . . *to be*

These participles and infinitives take on part time-jobs as **verbals**—parts of verbs that function not as verbs, but as adjectives, as adverbs, and even as nouns.

## Participle Phrases

Without the help of an auxiliary verb, participles simply work as **adjectives**; their function in a sentence, then, is to modify nouns and pronouns.

"I'm quite a *drinking man*," said Howard as he poured the tea.

The *deciding factor* in this competition was the swimsuit contest.

If the participle has accompanying it a group of related words, the whole is known as a **participle phrase**, which acts in a sentence as a stretched-out adjective.

*Grabbing the bat from the bat rack*, Robinson walked menacingly up to the mound.
It was a strange sight; the dog had a cigarette *dangling from its lip.*

## Infinitive Phrases

Where a participle may act only as an adjective, an infinitive can adapt its style to whatever context the writer places around it. An **infinitive phrase**, which consists of an infinitive plus its object (*to run a race, to sing an anthem*) can function as an **adjective**, an **adverb**, and even as a **noun**.

First, when an infinitive limits or modifies a noun or a pronoun, its role is that of an adjective:

We had no chance *to check our answers.* (*To check* modifies the noun *chance*.)
Floyd had money *to burn*. (*To burn* modifies the noun *money*.)

PARTS OF SPEECH

Second, when an infinitive modifies a verb, adjective, or adverb, its function is that of an adverb:

Paul ran *to save his life*. (*To save his life* tells us *why* he ran.)
Vanna helps the audience *to applaud at the right moment*.
(*To applaud* etc. tells us *how* she helps.)
We were anxious *to leave the country*. (*To leave* tells *why* we were anxious.)

Third, infinitives also have a non-modifying function; they can transform themselves into nouns to act as subjects, objects, or complements in a sentence.

*To know me* is *to love me*. (*to know me* = the subject/*to love me* = the subject complement)
Richard likes *to run* by the river. (*to run* = the direct object)

## Gerund Phrases

Whenever we deal with verbals, we must not forget the *gerund*, often confused with the participle. A gerund can never modify, but it carries the familiar **-ing** ending, thus resembling the present participle. Where participles act only as adjectives, a gerund can do anything a noun can do—act as a subject, direct object, complement, prepositional object:

*Eating* lemons can sour a personality.
(*Eating lemons* = gerund phrase acting as the subject of the sentence)

Compare the following sentences:

| GERUND | PARTICIPLE |
|---|---|
| *Crying* can often relieve tension. | The *crying* child nibbled its thumb. |
| I enjoy *listening* to Perry Como. | Beware of *listening* devices! |
| Sam got sore tonsils from *talking* too much. | *Talking* as he ate, Sam choked on his melon. |

| A SUMMARY: HOW VERBALS FUNCTION | | | |
|---|---|---|---|
| | ADJECTIVE | ADVERB | NOUN |
| PARTICIPLE | x | | |
| INFINITIVE | x | x | x |
| GERUND | | | x |

## Absolute Phrases

When a phrase appears to be doing more than its share of work by modifying not one word but the whole main clause, it is likely to be an **absolute phrase**. It is absolute because its job is to modify everything together rather than an isolated adjective, adverb, or noun in the clause:

Monica paced aimlessly about the room, *her heart pounding rapidly.*

A general rule for recognizing absolute phrases is to look especially for a noun or pronoun together with a participle; the phrase will be set off from the main clause by a comma:

*Stockmarket prices having fallen abruptly that morning,* Jackson trembled as he telephoned his broker.

# • Modifying Clauses

So far, we have been examining only **main clauses**—those grammatical entities that contain a subject, a predicate, and a complete thought. However, another type of clause is one whose role is as an accessory to the main clause; it qualifies as a clause because it contains a subject and a predicate, but its job is to modify rather than to express a complete idea. This type of clause is a **subordinate clause** because of its lesser importance. Subordinate clauses cannot stand on their own, and they are not generally essential to the functioning of the main clause.

Sometimes called **dependent clauses** because of their dependency on the main clause to make sense, subordinate clauses are not difficult to recognize. They usually telegraph their existence by beginning with a word that acts as a subordinate clause starter—a **subordinating conjunction** or a **relative pronoun**. Like adjective and adverb phrases, subordinate clauses have the job of modifying parts of the main clause; because of their modifying capabilities, they too act as "stretched-out" adjectives and adverbs.

## Clauses—What Are They?

A **clause** is a group of words containing a subject and predicate.

A **main clause** can make sense on its own; it is independent of other information in the sentence:

Ice cream is a delight to eat.

A **subordinate clause** cannot stand alone and make complete sense:

Although ice cream is a delight to eat . . .

PARTS OF SPEECH

It is dependent upon the sense of the main clause to which it is attached:

*Although ice cream is a delight to eat,* I must try to cut down my consumption of Butter Pecan to three bowls a day.

## Adjective Clauses

Like adjectives, adjective clauses modify nouns and pronouns. To identify them, look out for the relative pronouns/adjectives: *who, whom, which, that, whose.*

The stereo *that I bought on Saturday* has already been wrecked by my sister.
The man *whom you thought was my grandfather* is actually my husband.
Marriage, *which I never considered in my twenties,* has now become an attractive prospect.

In some instances, the relative pronoun may be omitted from an adjective clause:

The man *you thought was my grandfather* is my husband.
("That" is understood.)

## Adverb Clauses

Like their one-word counterparts, adverb clauses are able to modify verbs, adjectives, and adverbs and can generally answer the questions *how? when? where? how often? why?* and *on what condition?* They are introduced by any one of the following **subordinating conjunctions**:

| | | | |
|---|---|---|---|
| after* | because | that | whenever |
| although | before* | though | where |
| as* | if | unless | wherever |
| as if | since* | until* | whether |
| as though | so that | when | while |

*These words can also function as prepositions when they are followed by a noun or pronoun in a prepositional phrase.

*After I saw the movie "Splash,"* I couldn't eat a fishburger for months.
*Because John Wayne was the idol of millions,* Procter and Gamble asked him to do a detergent commercial.
Reading might be valuable *if you want to increase your vocabulary.*
Alice burped *whenever I tried to kiss her.*

CHAPTER ONE

Like one-word adverbs and adverb phrases, adverb clauses enjoy movement and are usually flexible as to where they are placed in a sentence:

I go *wherever you go.*        *Wherever you go,* I go.

### The Noun Clause

While we are on the subject of subordinate clauses, it is important to mention the type of clause that is not able to modify, but that can act as a subject, object, complement, or prepositional object—that can do anything that a noun can do: the **noun clause**.

*Where the boys are* is *where I want to be.* (Subject/Complement)
He assumed *that Victoria had no principles.* (Direct object)
The nurse showed great interest in *what the doctor said.*
(Prepositional object)

**NOTE:**  Remember that subordinate clauses cannot stand alone and that they rely on main clauses for their meaning. If you try to disguise a subordinate clause as a main clause by capitalizing it and ending it with a period the result will be a **sentence fragment** (see Chapter Three, p. 73).

## • The Appositive

Before we leave the subject of modifiers, it is appropriate to give recognition to the job of the **appositive**. The appositive fulfils just as important a role as its modifying colleague, the adjective.

The appositive—a single noun or a noun phrase—is not strictly a modifier, but its function nevertheless is to identify, describe, or add details to the noun or pronoun it follows:

George Brett, *the Kansas City third-baseman*, has a royal personality.
Wyatt Earp, *that no-good son-of-a-gun*, often ate cactus soup for the benefit of his eyesight.

# Connecting Words and Sentence Types •

## • Connecting Words

Words discussed in this section—prepositions, conjunctions and conjunctive adverbs—all have a common function: to connect. Some link only one noun to another, while others connect whole clauses. Each type has its own qualities and care must be taken not to confuse words belonging to one group of connectors with those belonging to another. For example, if you mistake the conjunctive adverb *however* for a coordinating conjunction, the result will be a **run-on sentence** (where two main clauses slither together because the writer has omitted to use either end punctuation or a connecting word correctly):

WRONG:  My grandmother had no formal education, however, she taught herself to read and write.

RIGHT:  My grandmother had no formal education, but she taught herself to read and write.

RIGHT:  My grandmother had no formal education; however, she taught herself to read and write.

(For more on run-on sentences, see Chapter Three p. 74. For the use of the semicolon, see Chapter Two p. 43.)

## Prepositions

**Prepositions** show the relationship between a noun or pronoun (the object of the preposition) and another word in the sentence. Prepositions often indicate location—*up, down, around, through, by, with, in, on*—and precede a noun or pronoun to form a prepositional phrase:

*up* the chimney                              *through* the hatch
*by* the door                                     *under* the rug

Prepositional phrases, whose job is always to modify, act as extended adjectives and adverbs. (See p. 28.)

## Coordinating Conjunctions

**Coordinating conjunctions** join words, phrases, or clauses of equal grammatical weight (nouns to nouns, participle phrases to participle phrases, main clauses to main clauses, etc.) Note that the coordinating conjunctions and the correlative conjunctions (see below) are the only connecting words that have the power to join main clauses.

Joining two nouns: beer *or* wine
Joining two prepositional phrases: laughing *and* crying
Joining two clauses: I may be blonde, *but* I'm not dumb.

The seven coordinating conjunctions are often referred to as the FAN-BOYS:

*For • And • Nor • But • Or • Yet • So*

(See also pp. 37, 47.)

CHAPTER ONE

## Correlative Conjunctions

**Correlative conjunctions** combine words, phrases or clauses of equal grammatical worth. Correlative conjunctions work in much the same way as the **FANBOYS** by combining equal parts, but they always work in pairs.

| | |
|---|---|
| both . . . and | I took *both* cash *and* credit cards on my shopping spree. |
| either . . . or | Eugene was *either* brilliant *or* insane; we couldn't tell. |
| neither . . . nor | The deer *neither* hid *nor* ran. It stood stock still. |
| not only . . . but also | We shall inform *not only* the dean *but also* your parents. |

## Subordinating Conjunctions

**Subordinating conjunctions** connect subordinate clauses to main clauses. Subordinating conjunctions (*although, since, when,* etc.) telegraph to the reader the lesser importance of the clauses that they precede:

I still call my mother for comfort *whenever things go wrong.*
Would you hurry up *so that we shall be on time*?

(See also p. 33.)

## Conjunctive Adverbs

**Conjunctive adverbs** indicate close relationships between main clauses. The following common conjunctive adverbs—

| | |
|---|---|
| accordingly | likewise |
| also | moreover |
| consequently | nevertheless |
| furthermore | then |
| however | therefore |
| instead | thus |

—cannot join main clauses, but they are able to signal a connection between two ideas and direct the reader's attention smoothly from the first clause to the second:

The sign by the pool proclaimed that the water was no more than six inches deep; *consequently*, it posed little danger to the children playing nearby.

(See also p. 43.)

REMEMBER: *However, then,* and *therefore* are not coordinating conjunctions; they cannot join main clauses.

# • Sentence Types

In the section on modifiers, you saw how five patterns of the simple sentence—the one-clause sentence—could be expanded and modified by the addition of subordinate clauses. (See p. 33.) Once you have learned how to distinguish between main and subordinate clauses in a sentence, you will also be able to classify the four **sentence types** according to the number and types of clauses that they contain. Being able to recognize the five patterns of the main clause and the four basic sentence types will help you to spot grammatical errors in your writing (such as comma errors and run-on sentences) and to vary your sentence structure.

### Type One: The Simple Sentence

The simple sentence contains one main clause.

John played rhythm guitar.

### Type Two: The Compound Sentence

The compound sentence contains two main clauses joined by a coordinating conjunction—one of the FANBOYS.

John played rhythm guitar, and Paul played bass.

### Type Three: The Complex Sentence

The complex sentence contains one main clause and one or more subordinate clauses.

While John played rhythm guitar, Paul played bass.

### Type Four: The Compound-complex Sentence

The compound-complex sentence contains two or more main clauses joined by a coordinating conjunction, together with one or more subordinate clauses.

While John played rhythm guitar, Paul played bass, George played lead guitar, and Ringo sang.

# Punctuation

"You got to mix them up, she showed? me "how to mix! them (and now; I can! mix up all kinds" of punctuation, in ! my writing? There, are lots! of rules? to lern; but Im gettin'g them in my head . . . (Punctuation, is; fun!)

Daniel Keyes,
From *Flowers for Algernon*, Mercury Press, 1959.

Punctuation makes clear the meaning of written language. Unpunctuated or improperly punctuated writing causes confusion since the reader can only guess what the writer meant. Mistakes, sometimes drastic ones, can happen.

Compare these two sentences:

Don't shoot Sgt. Lee until I give the command.
Don't shoot, Sgt. Lee, until I give the command.

Commas are not usually a matter of life and death, but here the difference that the commas make in these sentences can certainly affect Sgt. Lee's life.

Punctuation is, therefore, closely related to the meaning of the sentence. It signals pauses and stops. It stresses what is important and what is not. It

• 39 •

CHAPTER TWO

tells the reader what vocal inflections to use. Punctuation gives the reader directions. Many students follow this rule of thumb, *punctuate wherever you hear a pause*. This advice has some truth in it.

Unfortunately, however, a skilled writer cannot punctuate according to the way a speaker speaks. Anyone who includes all the pauses of speech will end up with superfluous punctuation. Using too much punctuation is just as distracting as using not enough.

The best practice is to punctuate to prevent misreading, following established rules. Once a writer becomes familiar with these rules, a range of choices becomes available: then punctuation can add to the writer's personal style or meaning.

# End Punctuation •

## • The Period

1. Use the **period** after a sentence which makes a statement, a request, an indirect question, or a mild command.

> Statement: Regina, your dog looks mean to me.
> Request: Please hold on to your dog until I close the gate.
> Indirect question: Kathy asked Regina if her dog attacked strangers.
> Mild command: Don't let that dog out yet.

2. Use the period after most **abbreviations**.

| | | | | |
|---|---|---|---|---|
| *Mr.* | *Ave.* | *A.D.* | *Jan.* | *lb.* |
| *Dr.* | *M.A.* | *i.e.* | *hr.* | *oz.* |

a. Abbreviations that are pronounced as words (acronyms) or spoken by the letters are usually written without periods. Many of them, like *radar*, have over the years become accepted words. *Radar*, for example, is the shortened form of **r**adio **d**etecting **a**nd **r**anging.

> NOW: National Organization for Women
> SALT: Strategic Arms Limitation Talks
> SONAR: Sound Navigation and Ranging
> USDA: United States Department of Agriculture
> IRS: Internal Revenue Service
> USSR: Union of Soviet Social Republics

**NOTE:** Do not use a period after U.S. Post Office abbreviations of states. When in doubt consult a recent dictionary.

PUNCTUATION

CA: California     MA: Massachusetts

**b.** If a declarative sentence ends with an abbreviation, use only one period. Don't fall into the "if one is good, two must be better" trap.

> Mildred and Ramon Garcia were delighted with the birth of their first son, Ramon Garcia, Jr.

**c.** If an interrogative or exclamatory sentence ends with an abbreviation, place the question mark or the exclamation point after the period.

> Where did Roland receive his Ph.D.?
> Fritz has two classes that start at 8:00 a.m.!

**d.** If an abbreviation is placed within a sentence, use the period along with the punctuation marks that would normally be used.

> My check was made payable to Terence Wilmer, Ph.D., my therapist.

**3.** Use the period in decimals, the metric system, and with currency notation.

> 2.7809  0.375  cc.  $575.32  1.89  3.36  F.F.  $0.95  5.63%  4.52  kg.

# • The Question Mark

**1.** Use the **question mark** after a direct question.

> Ma'am, will you please call off your dog?

Do not, however, use the question mark after an indirect question.

> I asked the old lady next door if she would call her dog.

**2.** Use the question mark also after a rhetorical question, a question that does not require or expect a reply.

> Mother says to child: "Don't you think it's about time for you to go to bed?"
> I wasn't going to buy that dress—do you think I'm crazy?

**3.** Use the question mark after a quizzical comment.

> You think she's weird?
> You want to blame me for this mess?

CHAPTER TWO

4. Use the question mark after a series of questions in the same sentence.

> As I flew through the windshield, I thought, "Is this it? Am I going to die? Did I pay the insurance?"

5. Use the question mark in parentheses to show that information might be inexact.

> The first wrestling match (46 B.C.?) was recorded in Japan.

## • The Exclamation Point

Use the **exclamation point** after a single word that expresses strong feeling—this is also known as an **interjection**—or after a sentence that expresses strong emotion.

> Ouch!
> Your dog bit me!

**NOTE:** An interjection at the beginning of a sentence is usually followed by a comma, not an exclamation point.

> Oh, I've spilled the beer all over your pants.
> Well, look who finally showed up!

## • Common Errors to Avoid in End Punctuation

1. Avoid the overuse of the exclamation point. You can't turn a dull sentence or a dull paragraph into an exciting one by adding exclamation points one after another.

> John is so terrific!!!!
>    I went to a dance last night! John was there! He was dancing with Sue! He's broken up with Heather! And, he is going to the beach with me tomorrow! I could just die of excitement!

**P.S.** The reader died of boredom.

**NOTE:** In the following passage the writer creates excitement without resorting to the exclamation point.

> Junior backed up against the school yard wall. The punks crowded around him. He felt fear—not fear of them. He was afraid of what he might do. One of them spit on him. Junior's fear disappeared with a

shrug. With a sweep of his hand, the ground opened and swallowed them whole.

2. Do not use more than one end punctuation mark at the end of a sentence.

> WRONG: John asked, "What time shall I pick you up?".
> RIGHT: John asked, "What time shall I pick you up?"
> WRONG: Who said, "I came; I saw; I conquered."?
> RIGHT: Who said, "I came; I saw; I conquered"?

# Internal Punctuation •

## • The Semicolon

The **semicolon** lies between the comma and the period in strength and length of pause. The comma separates and encloses words, phrases, and clauses; the period separates and terminates sentences. The semicolon separates main clauses within a sentence, often eliminating a conjunction. Its use implies that the two main clauses are closely related. If you are in doubt, use the period; it's always a safe choice.

1. Use the semicolon between main clauses that are closely realted in thought.

> Our coach can hardly wait for the new season to start; his new center is seven feet tall.
> Take only what you absolutely need; you may have to carry it all on your back.

2. Use the semicolon between main clauses joined by a conjunctive adverb. (See p. 36.) The conjunctive adverbs are

| | | |
|---|---|---|
| accordingly | henceforth | namely |
| also | however* | nevertheless |
| anyhow | in addition | otherwise |
| as a result | indeed | similarly |
| besides | in fact | still |
| consequently | instead | surely |
| finally | likewise | then* |
| furthermore | meanwhile | therefore* |
| hence | moreover | thus |

*The three most often misused conjunctive adverbs.

**NOTE:** If the introductory conjunctive adverb is several syllables long (*however, as a result*, etc.), it is usually followed by a comma.

Student issues were to be discussed; therefore, the student council was invited to attend.

After short conjunctive adverbs (*thus*, *then*, etc.) the comma is often omitted.

Student issues were discussed; then coffee was served.

3. Use the semicolon between main clauses joined by a coordinating conjunction if there are several commas within the clauses. The coordinating conjunctions are *for*, *and*, *nor*, *but*, *or*, *yet*, *so*. (Remember the FANBOYS).

Our coach, who lost most of his games last season, can hardly wait for the new one to start; for his new center, a freshman, is seven feet, two inches tall.
You'll have to carry all your equipment on your back—the tent, the canoe, which you had better not forget, and your extra clothing; so take only what you absolutely need.

4. Use the semicolon to separate a series of items if the items contain commas.

The new music group consists of John, the saxophonist; Miriam, the lead singer; Jim, the guitarist; and Kelly, the drummer.

5. Do **not** use the semicolon to separate a main clause from a dependent clause or from a phrase. Use a comma instead.

WRONG: Although student issues were to be discussed; the student council was not invited to attend.
RIGHT: Although student issues were to be discussed, the student council was not invited to attend.

## •  The Colon

The **colon** is a rather formal mark of punctuation that introduces words, phrases or clauses that explain, illustrate, or amplify the first part of the sentence. A grammatically complete clause or a sentence must precede the clause.

WRONG: A well-balanced meal should consist of: milk, meat, vegetable, cereal, and fruit.
RIGHT: My diet consists of generous portions from five basic food groups: salt, sugar, fat, alcohol, and starch.

PUNCTUATION

1. Use the colon to introduce a list of items, especially after *as follows* and *the following*.

> To apply for the job, please proceed as follows: 1) read the application carefully; 2) complete the application form; 3) mail the finished application to Washington.

2. Use the colon to introduce a long, formal statement or quotation.

> Voltaire was never fair in his treatment of Leibnitz: "Leibnitz sensed there was nothing to be said in reply, and so he made big fat books in which he confused himself."

3. Use the colon to separate main clauses when the second clause explains or identifies the first.

> His biggest problem is women: John wants all of them.

**NOTE:** Do not use a capital letter after the colon unless what follows is a sentence. If you are unsure whether or not to use the colon to separate main clauses, use the period.

4. Use the colon to mark conventional separations.

   **a.** Hours from minutes: *11:45*
      Proportions and ratios: *3:4  6:8*

   **b.** Chapter from verse in the Bible: *Timothy 2:3*

   **c.** Volume from pages: *212: 46–47*
      Act from scene: *Hamlet, II:4*

   **d.** Title and subtitle: *Writing: Process and Structure*

   **e.** Place from publisher: *New York: Harper and Row*

5. Use the colon after formal salutations, especially in the business letter.

> Dear Parent:
> Dear Senator Dodd:
> Gentlemen:
> To Whom It May Concern:

6. Do **not** use the colon between verbs and their complements, between prepositions and their objects, and after *such as* or *for example*.

   **a.** Between verbs and complements:

> WRONG: The band needs: a flutist, a second violinist, two oboists, and a drummer.

RIGHT: The band needs the following: a flutist, a second violinist, two oboists, and a drummer.
WRONG: The only jobs available are: waiter, car washer, cashier, and dishwasher.
RIGHT: The only jobs available are as follows: waiter, car washer, cashier, and dishwasher.

**b.** Prepositions and their objects:

WRONG: Applications should be sent to: Student Admissions.
RIGHT: Applications should be sent to Student Admissions.

**c.** *Such as* or *for example*:

WRONG: The disaster victims still need items such as: blankets, tents, clothing, canned food, and drinking water.
RIGHT: The disaster victims still need items such as blankets, tents, clothing, canned food, and drinking water.

# • The Comma

The basic function of the **comma** is to help make the meaning of a sentence clear. It indicates the degree of pause or emphasis or the importance of a relationship between words, clauses, and phrases to the rest of the sentence. Of the internal punctuation marks—commas, semicolons, colons, dashes, and parentheses—the comma has the widest variety of uses and demands the slightest pause and emphasis.

Comma use can be simplified by dividing it into three general areas:
(1) Commas group words that belong together.
(2) Commas separate those that do not.
(3) Commas are used for conventional purposes that have little to do with meaning.

## Series

Use the comma to separate words, phrases, or clauses in a series of three or more elements of equal rank.

The last two elements of the series are usually joined by *and* or *or*. A comma before the *and* or *or* may often be omitted, especially in informal or journalistic writing.

**1.** Series of nouns:

The school band desperately needs a trombone, a Sousaphone, a piccolo, and a triangle.

**2.** Series of verbs:

> The soprano expanded her rib cage, opened her mouth, drew a deep breath, and coughed.

**3.** Series of prepositional phrases:

> The children dashed from the car, over the boardwalk, toward the beach, and into the waves.

**4.** Series of short clauses:

> The pianist pounded, the soprano screeched, and the audience left.

**NOTE:** If all the elements in a series are joined by *and* or *or*, do not use the comma to separate them.

> The angry student felt frustrated and betrayed and very bitter.
> Young lady, you are grounded this entire weekend; that means you can't go to the movies or to the dance or to basketball practice.

## Main Clauses Joined by Coordinating Conjunction

Use the comma to separate main clauses joined by a coordinating conjunction. Place a comma before the coordinating conjunctions *for, and, nor, but, or, yet, so,* (the FANBOYS) unless the clauses are very short.

**1.** With short clauses, the comma is not necessary.

> COMMA REQUIRED: The mailman delivered several letters, but he didn't bring a single one for me.
> NO COMMA REQUIRED: Charlie fidgeted and Maria endured.

**2.** When the clauses are internally punctuated with commas, use a semicolon before the coordinating conjunction to separate the clauses. Comma punctuation is not enough. (See Semicolons p. 44.)

> The street musicians, dressed in black and white harlequin costumes, played all day at the downtown shopping mall; but the sword swallowers, fire-eaters, and shell game artists collected the money the musicians should have received.

## Consecutive Adjectives

Use the comma to separate two or more consecutive adjectives that precede the noun they both modify.

> He played the role of the surly, suffering, and searching artist.

**1.** Do not use a comma between the final adjective and the noun.

The large blond woman wore a frilly, pink dress.

**NOTE:** Do not use a comma between the adverb and the adjective that it modifies.

The large blond woman wore a dark pink dress.

The adverb *dark* modifies the adjective *pink*, not the noun *dress*, so no comma should be used.

**2.** Commas are often omitted with numerals and with adjectives of size and age.

ten little children
my lazy old dog
your fat black cat

## Misreading

Use the comma to separate words or phrases that might be misread.

Before starting to eat, the dog ran around in circles.

(This might otherwise be read as *Before starting to eat the dog. . . .*)

For Sue, Ellen was a threat to any male friend she might have.

## Ellipsis

Use the comma to indicate an ellipsis in a sentence when the structure of the sentence makes clear what is omitted. An ellipsis indicates that words that are obviously understood have been omitted.

My coat is rabbit, hers mink.
The Hulls are leaving for Vienna; we, for Amsterdam.

## Introductory Elements

Use the comma to separate introductory elements which precede the main clauses, especially when the introductory element is not essential to the meaning of the independent clause.

**1.** Introductory words: mild exclamation or direct address

Well, no one told me about this!
No, I won't.
Kathy, are you still fiddling with that computer?

PUNCTUATION

**2.** Participle phrase modifying the subject (see p. 30):

Having been roasted, the chicken was ready for eating.

**NOTE:** The introductory participle phrase must modify the subject to prevent the dangling modifier. (See p. 94.)

Having been roasted, the cook served the chicken.

*Having been roasted,* in this case, places the cook in a hot spot he or she most certainly would like to avoid.

**3.** Absolute phrase: an absolute phrase is a noun or pronoun joined with a present or past participle and used as a modifier for the entire clause rather than a particular word. (See p. 32.)

Present Participle: *His mouth hanging open*, the sleeping student snorted once and jerked himself awake.
Past Participle: *Her tail wound neatly around her front paws*, the cat watched the soccer game on television.

**4.** Long prepositional phrase (five words or longer):

At the edge of the burnt forest, the exhausted fire fighters surveyed the damage.

**5.** Short prepositional phrase which is **not** essential to the main clause. Such phrases usually function as transitions.

In addition, the thief took my best pair of jeans. On the other hand, all the jewelry he took was fake.

**NOTE:** Short prepositional phrases that are essential to the main clause should never be separated with a comma.

Without my morning coffee I am never wide awake.

**6.** Adverb clause:

As I packed our suitcases, the cat watched me intently.

**NOTE:** Usually, an adverb clause at the end of a sentence is not set off with commas.

The cat watched me intently as I packed our suitcases.

CHAPTER TWO

## Non-essential Expressions

Use the comma to set off **non-essential expressions** that interrupt the structure of the sentence.

A non-essential expression is a modifier which is not absolutely necessary to the basic meaning of the sentence. It merely adds information to the sentence. This modifier, or interrupter, could be a word, a phrase, or a clause.

> WORD: Diane Flatten, *flutist*, won a scholarship to the Julliard School of Music.
> PHRASE: Diane Flatten, *our best flutist*, won a scholarship to the Julliard School of Music.
> CLAUSE: Diane Flatten, *who is the school's best flutist*, won a scholarship to the Julliard School of Music.

**NOTE:** *Flutist, our best flutist,* or *who is the school's best flutist* merely adds information to the sentence. It is non-essential to the meaning of the sentence. Because it interrupts the basic structure of the sentence, it is set off with two commas. If the word, phrase, or clause had come first or last in the sentence, then only one comma would have been needed.

> The Julliard School of Music awarded a scholarship to Diane Flatten, *our flutist.*

Deciding whether a modifier is essential or non-essential is not always easy, but it can be vital in communicating your meaning. Consider the following sentence, punctuated with and without commas to set off the modifying clause:

> NON-ESSENTIAL MODIFIER: Adult students, *who hold full-time jobs*, often must juggle conflicting responsibilities in order to further their education. (The use of commas indicates that sentence refers to adult students in general.)

> ESSENTIAL MODIFIER: Adult students who hold full-time jobs often must juggle conflicting responsibilities in order to further their education. (Lack of commas indicates that only *working adult students* are under discussion.)

**NOTE:** Non-essential and essential expressions are sometimes referred to as **non-restrictive** and **restrictive** elements. An essential expression should **not** be set off by commas since it is a modifier that is necessary to the basic meaning of the sentence. It identifies its antecedent—the element it follows—as a particular group, person, thing, or idea.

If the essential expression, *who hold full-time jobs*, is removed from the above sentence, the basic meaning of the sentence is altered.

Adult students often must juggle conflicting responsibilities in order to further their education.

1. Use commas to set off **non-essential appositives**. An appositive is a noun or noun phrase with or without modifiers that immediately follows another noun or pronoun and identifies or explains it. (See Chapter One, p. 34).

Dr. Buchner, *a physicist at the university*, plays the flute in a chamber music ensemble.

**NOTE:** An essential appositive should not be set off with commas.

The satirist Swift tried to correct the ills of eighteenth-century England.
Frederick the Great enlisted giants as his bodyguards.

2. Use commas to set off **parenthetical expressions**. Parenthetical expressions interrupt the normal flow of the sentence.

a. Conjunctive adverbs:

Hamilton, however, was never elected President.
Anselm, likewise, will be arriving late.

b. Parenthetical comments:

Beer, of course, is the liquid of life.
The critic's evaluation of his performance, I think, was totally fair.

c. Qualifying words and phrases:

Cats, especially Siamese cats, often display far more intelligence than dogs do.
Her clothes, elegant and expensive, were very simple.

d. Direct address:

I don't know, Rosie, where Charlie is.
It's time, Fritz, to get up.

## Dialogue Guide

Use the comma with the **dialogue guide**. The dialogue guide is a clause such as *he asked, she commented,* or *they thought* which indicates that the writer is citing a person's exact words.

> Isabel asked, "When shall I pick you up tonight?"
> "I am going to Vienna to the carnival," he said with determination, "even if I have to miss class to do it."
> "We'll start the program in ten minutes," announced Anita.

## Conventional Situations

Use the comma in established **conventional situations**.

**1.** Addresses:

> Aunt Marge's address is 89 Thayer Street, New York, NY 10040.
> Send your application to The University of Maryland, College Park, MD 20742.

**NOTE:** A comma separates the street from the city and the city from the state. No comma is used to separate the zip code.

**2.** Dates:

> Charlie's father was born on July 4, 1914.
> In December, 1941, the United States entered World War II.

**NOTE:** The comma is sometimes omitted between the month and the year.

> In December 1941, the United States entered World War II.

**NOTE:** When military or continental style is used, no comma is required.

> Charlie's father was born on 4 July 1914.

**3.** Titles and degrees:

> Warren Bellamy Shull, Ph.D.
> Charles Newkirk, Sr.
> Anthony Armstrong Hadley, IV

**NOTE:** If a name followed by a title is used within a sentence, a comma should be used between the title and the rest of the sentence as well.

> Charles Newkirk, Sr., was elected to the Board of Directors, Texaco.

PUNCTUATION

**4.** Names reversed:

> Gropius, Walter
> Schellkopf, Fritz

**5.** Statistics:

> On October 19th, Black Monday, the volume on the Big Board was as much as 200,000,000 shares in excess of the computers' ability to handle it.
> The new basketball center is seven feet, two inches.

**NOTE:** The comma is sometimes omitted in four digit numbers.

> There are 2000 English expressions that describe drunkeness.

**6.** Salutation and complimentary closing in informal letters:

> Dear Jane and Boris,
> With love,
> Affectionately,

# • The Dash

The **dash** sets off supplementary information with emphasis or indicates a dramatic break in thought. Use the dash to signal a pause longer and more dramatic than a comma. Use the dash for emphasis, but remember that like stage make-up, a little is very effective; too much is overwhelming. When typing the dash, use two hyphens without leaving any space before and after. The handwritten dash is the length of two letters.

**1.** Use the dash to indicate a sudden break or interruption in thought.

> My first impression of her—and I was only twelve at the time—was that she was everything that I wanted to be.

**2.** Use the dash to set off with emphasis a parenthetical or explanatory element.

> My five basic food groups—salt, fat, sugar, starch, and alcohol—will bring about my early funeral.

**3.** Use the dash to set off an introductory list or series.

> The VCR, microwave oven, home computer, and robot—these are the indicators that we have moved into the electronic age.

**4.** Use the dash to indicate a break or hesitation in thought or speech.

Those pants—uh—well, I—think they're a bit—uh—ugly.

**5.** Use the dash to indicate an unfinished sentence.

"Please, don't do—" her voice failed.

**6.** Use the dash to indicate an omission of letters in a word.

Mayor W— was accused of bribery and drug peddling.

# • Parentheses

**Parentheses**, like commas and dashes, set off supplementary information; however, they indicate that the information is unimportant to the main idea of the sentence or paragraph. Parentheses () are always used in pairs.

**1.** Use the parentheses to enclose incidental, explanatory material that is unimportant or unnecessary to the main idea of the sentence.

Senator Edward Kennedy (Dem.—Massachusetts) is the brother of the late President John F. Kennedy.
Combustion (the burning of gases) in the cylinders causes the pistons to move.
The trend marks a sharp increase (Table 3) in the rise of unemployment in large cities.

**2.** Use the parentheses to enclose numbers or letters noting divisions included within the text of a sentence or within a paragraph.

The two companies might be compared in terms of (1) their involvement in Third World countries' politics, (2) their production of material harmful to the environment, and (3) their hiring practices.

Puberty changes can be observed in (a) growth of hair, (b) change in voice, and (c) increase in hormone action.

**NOTE:** Commas, dashes, and parentheses—these are the three punctuation marks that set off supplementary information: (1) the most commonly used marks, commas, set off material that is closely related to the main idea of the sentence; (2) the dashes—creating a dramatic break—emphasize more strongly what they set off; and (3) the parentheses (indicating a distant relationship) lessen the importance of the matter that they set off.

# • The Apostrophe

The **apostrophe** is used to show possession, to indicate the omission of letters from words or figures from numerals, or to form the plurals of letters, numbers, or words.

### Possessive Case

Use the apostrophe to show the **possessive case** of nouns and indefinite pronouns.

1. For words ending in s, simply add the apostrophe after the s. These words may be singular or plural.

| SINGULAR NOUNS | PLURAL NOUNS |
|---|---|
| princess' wedding | ten cents' worth |
| scissors' blade | two weeks' salary |
| witness' immunity | seven years' time |
| Achilles' tendon | Smiths' house |
| Charles' house | parents' marriage |
| Mars' canals | ladies' room |
| Degas' dancers | enemies' attack |

2. For words **not** ending in s, simply add 's. These words may be singular or plural.

| SINGULAR NOUNS | PLURAL NOUNS |
|---|---|
| cat's whiskers | men's coats |
| child's life | children's rights |
| goose's liver | geese's feathers |
| today's society | data's source |
| year's end | mice's nests |
| Ms. Steinem's book | teeth's caries |
| bachelor's degree | alumni's dance |

**NOTE:** For indefinite pronouns (see Chapter One, p. 23) simply add 's.

| | | |
|---|---|---|
| nobody's business | one's position | anyone's job |
| another's interest | somebody's keys | nobody's home |
| no one's fault | everybody's benefits | neither's fault |

3. To show possession in compound words (those with hyphens), terms of joint possession, and names of organizations, use the apostrophe only with the last word.

CHAPTER TWO

| | |
|---|---|
| mother-in-law's car | Jack and Jill's pail |
| editor-in-chief's job | Jackson Five's hit record |
| Johnson and Johnson's ad campaign | Boston Symphony's conductor |
| Internal Revenue Service's ruling | Karen and Christoff's party |

**4.** To show individual possession in compound words, use the apostrophe with each element.

Army's and Navy's regulations          Kim's and Bill's cars

## Omission

Use the apostrophe to indicate the **omission of letters** or numbers.

**1.** Omission of letters in contractions: a contraction is made up of two words joined together to form a single word by omitting one or more letters. Be sure to place the apostrophe exactly where the letters are omitted.

| | |
|---|---|
| it's (it is) | o'clock (of the clock) |
| I'll (I shall; I will) | can't (cannot) |
| where's (where is) | they're (they are) |
| doesn't (does not) | mustn't (must not) |
| they've (they have) | we'd (we had or we would) |
| OK'd (okayed) | won't (will not) |
| George'll (George will) | would've (would have) |

**NOTE:**  Do not confuse the possessive pronoun, *its*, with *it's* (it is).

**REMEMBER:** Contractions usually reflect spoken usage. Because they are informal, they are rarely appropriate in formal, expository writing.

**2.** Omission of letters in reproducing dialogue:

"Ma'am, he ain't goin' nowhere t'day."
" 'ow can'e do theeze to me?"

**3.** Omission of numbers:

Spirit of '76
Class of '63

## Plurals

Use the apostrophe to form the plurals of letters, numbers, abbreviations or acronyms, symbols, and words referred to within a sentence.

**1.** Plural of letters:

> Anyone who gets all A's and B's in Mrs. Hull's class is a genius.

**2.** Plurals of numbers:

> The 1920's and the 1950's are the decades we copy the most.

**3.** Plurals of acronyms:

> The Americans and the Russians have a comparable number of ICBM's.

**4.** Plurals of symbols:

> When the key changes, don't forget to play those F#'s.

**5.** Plural of words used as entities:

> You start too many of your sentences with *he*'s.

## Incorrect Usage

Do **not** use the apostrophe in these cases:

> Plural nouns that are not in the possessive case.

Do not confuse plural and possessive.

> WRONG: The Mitchum's spend their vacations at Niagara Falls.
> RIGHT: The Mitchums spend their vacations at Niagara Falls.

Verbs that end in **s**. Adding an apostrophe does not make these verb forms either possessive or plural.

> WRONG: Charles jog's and swim's every day.
> RIGHT: Charles jogs and swims every day.

Possessive pronouns: *his, hers, its, ours, yours, theirs. Its*—without the apostrophe—is a pronoun form like *his* and *hers*. Do not use an apostrophe with it unless you intend to use the expression *it is*.

> WRONG: The cat left its' mouse in my shoe.
> RIGHT: The cat left its mouse in my shoe.

CHAPTER TWO

# • Quotation Marks

Quotation marks, both double and single, are used to set off from a writer's own words the direct speech or written material quoted word by word from another source. Double quotation marks are placed at the beginning and the end of quoted material. Single quotation marks are generally used to enclose quoted material within a quotation. On occasion, single quotation marks are used in some books, magazines and newspapers instead of double quotation marks.

1. Use quotation marks to set off a person's exact words in a direct quotation.

> The teacher said, "The student can't spell."
> "The teacher," said the student, "can't spell."

**NOTE:** Do not use quotation marks to set off an indirect quotation.

> The teacher said that the student couldn't spell.

2. Use the single quotation mark to set off a quotation within a quotation.

> The principal complained, "The student said, 'The teacher can't spell.'"

3. Use the indentation method when quoting a long passage. Set the quotation off from the rest of the paper with indentations of at least a half inch and single spacing. In this case, no quotation marks are necessary.

> Truman Capote presents memories of Christmas in a language of the senses:
>> The black stove, stoked with coal and firewood, glows like a lighted pumpkin. Eggbeaters whirl, spoons spin round in bowls of butter and sugar, vanilla sweetens the air, ginger spices it; melting, nose-tingling odors saturate the kitchen, suffuse the house, drift out to the world on puffs of chimney smoke. (Truman Capote, *A Christmas Memory*)

4. Use quotation marks to set off titles of articles, chapters, short stories, poems, songs, radio and television programs, and subdivisions of books and periodicals.

> The first article I turn to in *Harper's* is the "Harper's Index."

PUNCTUATION

> One of the students ran out of the classroom when we read Swift's "A Modest Proposal."

**NOTE:** Do not use quotation marks to set off the title of your student theme when you place it at the top of your paper.

5. Use quotation marks to set off slang words, technical jargon, or words used in an ironic sense.

> Kurt's thinking is all "screwed-up"!
> Werner Heisenberg won the Nobel Prize for his "uncertainty principle."
> You call this "good" writing?

**NOTE:** Use this device sparingly. Do not use quotation marks as the excuse to use slang words because you cannot think of or won't be bothered to find the appropriate one.

6. When quoting material, **capitalize** according to established conventions.

   a. Capitalize the first letter of a sentence in the direct quotation.

   > The teacher said, "The student can't spell."

   b. Do not capitalize the second part of a sentence divided by an interrupting dialogue guide.

   > WRONG: "The teacher," said the student, "Can't spell."
   > RIGHT: "The teacher," said the student, "can't spell."

   c. Capitalize the first letter of the second half of a quotation if a new sentence begins the quotation.

   > "The teacher can't spell," said the student. "She makes mistakes on the board all the time."

   d. Do not capitalize the first letter of a quoted fragment integrated into a sentence.

   > The expression "straight from the horse's mouth" comes to us from horse dealers' jargon.

7. When quoting material, follow conventional usage regarding other marks of punctuation.

   a. Use the comma, generally, to set off the dialogue guide.

CHAPTER TWO

> She screamed in exultation, "I won!"
> "You might erase the whole program," she warned.
> "Where," he asked, "is your mother?"

**b.** Place commas and periods inside quotation marks.

> After reading "The Lottery," the class discussed the themes
> evident in the story.
> Drinking bottled water, white wine, or imported beer is "in."

**c.** Place semicolons and colons outside quotation marks.

> Gertrude Stein wrote, "Commas are servile and they have no life of
> their own"; she did not pay much attention to them.

**d.** Place the question mark and exclamation point outside the quotation marks if the *whole* sentence demands the question mark or the exclamation point.

> Did John say, "I'll pick you up at nine"?
> John said, "Shall I pick you up at nine?"
> Diane screamed, "Something's moving in my boot!"
> Stop screaming "I told you so"!

**e.** Use only one end punctuation mark when it can apply to both the quotation and the whole sentence.

> The job interviewer asked, "Do you smoke?"

**8.** When writing dialogue, begin a new paragraph with each change of speaker.

> "It's pretty hot." the man said.
> "Let's drink beer."
> "Dos cervezas," the man said into the curtain.
> "Big ones?" a woman asked from the doorway.
> "Yes. Two big ones."

> > Ernest Hemingway,
> > From "Hills Like White Elephants"

**NOTE:** When one speaker's dialogue continues for more than one paragraph, place quotation marks at the beginning of each paragraph, but not at the end. The closing quotation marks are placed only at the end of the entire quoted passage.

PUNCTUATION

"My bride's mother I had never seen: I understood she was dead. The honeymoon over, I learned my mistake; she was only mad, and shut up in a lunatic asylum. There was a younger brother, too—a complete dumb idiot. The elder one, whom you have seen (and whom I cannot hate, whilst I abhor all his kindred, because he has some grains of affection in his feeble mind, shown in the continued interest he takes in his wretched sister, and also in a dog-like attachment he once bore me), will probably be in the same state one day. My father and my brother Rowland knew all this; but they thought only of the thirty thousand pounds, and joined in the plot against me.

. . . .

"Jane, I will not trouble you with abominable details; some strong words shall express what I have to say. I lived with that woman upstairs four years, and before that time she had tried me indeed: her character ripened and developed with frightful rapidity; her vices sprang up fast and rank: they were so strong, only cruelty could check them, and I would not use cruelty. What a pigmy intellect she had, and what giant propensities! How fearful were the curses those propensities entailed on me! Bertha Mason, the true daughter of an infamous mother, dragged me through all the hideous and degrading agonies which must attend a man bound to a wife at once intemperate and unchaste.

"My brother in the interval was dead, and at the end of the four years my father died, too. I was rich enough now—yet poor to hideous indigence: a nature the most gross, impure, depraved I ever saw, was associated with mine, and called by the law and by society a part of me. And I could not rid myself of it by any legal proceedings: for doctors now discovered that *my wife* was mad—her excesses had prematurely developed the germs of insanity. Jane, you don't like my narrative; you look almost sick—shall I defer the rest to another day?"

Charlotte Brontë,
From *Jane Eyre*

# • The Hyphen

The hyphen is used to divide words, to form compound words and numbers, and to add prefixes, suffixes, and letters to words. Because our language is constantly changing, check a dictionary to see if a once-hyphenated word has become one word, e.g. *nonsense, baseball, rainwater*.

1. Use the hyphen to divide a multisyllable word at the end of a line. Words should be divided according to syllables. Consult a dictionary for accepted division. Dots divide the words into syllables (syl.la.ble). Do not divide a one-syllable word.

   John's brother is working in Argentina as a trans-
   portation expert.

**2.** Use the hyphen to form compound words.

> brother-in-law   sergeant-major   attorney-at-law

**3.** Use the hyphen with prefixes, suffixes, and letters that form a coined word.

> pro-Reagan voter           all-American athlete
> anti-rust paint            self-imposed exile
> Pan-Hellenic games         president-elect
> T-shirt                    x-ray

**4.** Use the hyphen to connect two or more words serving as a single adjective before a noun.

> rosy-fingered dawn         gray-eyed beauty

If the first word ends in **-ly**, do not use the hyphen.

> harshly spoken words       steely eyed killer

If the expression follows the verb as a predicative adjective, do not use the hyphen.

> Athena, our cat, was green eyed.

**5.** Use the hyphen to prevent confusion or awkwardness.

> re-cover (to prevent confusion with *recover*)
> re-collect (to prevent confusion with *recollect*)
> re-form (to prevent confusion with *reform*)
> shell-like (to prevent awkwardness of three l's in *shelllike*)
> anti-intellectual (to prevent the double vowel—*antiintellectual*)

**6.** Use the hyphen to form nonce or one-time-only compounds.

> I hate her you're-so-dumb look.
> I could hear the clop-clop of horses' hooves.

**7.** Use the hyphen to form numbers from twenty-one to ninety-nine, fractions used as adjectives, and ratios.

> forty-four                 ten one-thousandths of an inch
> three-fourths cup          thirty-two twenty-fourths
> twenty-twenty vision       forty-first state

**NOTE:** When a fraction is used as a noun, do not use the hyphen.

PUNCTUATION

I lost one half of my salary playing black jack.

8. Use the hyphen between numbers and units of measure.

6-inch ruler                    50-minute hour
40-hour week                    20-pound load

9. Use the hyphen to indicate hesitation in speech.

Porky Pig called out, "Y-y-yes, I'm c-coming."

# • Ellipsis

The **ellipsis**, a series of three spaced periods, indicates that one or more words have been omitted from a quoted passage. If one or more sentences are omitted, four spaced periods are used. A writer might use ellipsis either to save space or to focus on a particular idea contained in the quoted passage.

Ellipsis can also be used to indicate that a statement or a listing continues beyond the words or items given.

1. Use the ellipsis of three spaced periods to indicate that one or more words have been omitted intentionally from a direct quotation. Use a fourth period to indicate the end of an omitted sentence.

ORIGINAL PASSAGE:

From the topics assigned, one can safely assume that what the teacher wanted from these students was a *descriptive* essay. He or she would probably have explained further that the first topic—the seashore in summer—lends itself well to *static description*, and that the second subject—an evening's experiences in the student union—allows scope for an essay developed by narration, one of the most common types of *dynamic description*.

PASSAGE WITH OMISSIONS:

From the topics assigned, . . . the teacher wanted . . . a *descriptive* essay. . . . the first topic—the seashore in summer—lends itself well to static description, and . . . the second subject—an evening's experiences in the student union—allows scope for . . . narration. . . .

2. Use the ellipsis to indicate the continuation of a statement or an enumeration.

"Count to ten," she said.
"One, two, three . . ." I began.

## • Brackets

**Brackets** are used to enclose the writer's comment or explanation that is inserted in a quoted passage.

1. Use brackets to set off comments added within quoted material. The brackets indicate that you, the writer, are commenting on the original material.

> "Be certain there have been no truly good kings except those who began like you [Frederick the Great] by educating themselves, by learning to know men, by loving the truth, by detesting persecution and superstition."
>
> Voltaire

2. Use brackets to set off corrections you wish to add to the original or with **[sic]** to draw attention to an error.

> "The Constitution was signed in 1786 [1787]."
> "I get awful headaches and sperin [sic] doesnt help much."
>
> Daniel Keyes,<br>From *Flowers for Algernon*, Mercury Press, 1959.

The word [sic] indicates that the mistake in spelling or grammar in the quoted material appears in the original text. **Sic** means "just as it is."

## • The Slash or Virgule

The **slash** or **virgule** indicates alternatives. In technical writing it may be used as a dividing line to separate numerals, letters and words. It also serves to separate lines of poetry quoted within the text of a prose passage.

1. Use the slash or virgule to indicate alternatives.

> and/or   he/she   hers/his

2. Use the slash or virgule as dividing line in dates, fractions, and to stand for *per* or *in the case of* in technical and business writing.

> 3/10/65   3/4   55 miles/hour   c/o

3. Use the slash or virgule to act as a dividing line in two or more lines of poetry quoted within a prose text. (The virgule marks the end of the line as it appears in the poem.)

> A. E. Housman's famous poem "To an Athlete Dying Young" begins with the following lines: "The time you won your town the race/We chaired you through the market place."

# • Numbers

1. Spell out numbers that can be expressed in one or two reasonable words; use figures for the others.

> I spent twenty-two hours writing my paragraph for her!
> Fred finds 358 reasons for not turning in his paper on time.

Business and technical writers generally use figures for numbers above ten.

2. Spell out numbers that occur at the beginning of a sentence.

> Two hundred years ago, Mozart played billiards on this very table.

3. Spell out a fraction when it is used alone.

> Agatha spends more than two-thirds of her salary on make-up.

4. Use figures for the following:

   a. Addresses to include room or apartment numbers, and postal zone:

   > 12 Rustic Avenue, Apt. 3G
   > Groton, MA 01450
   > 415 Sutter Street, Room 34
   > San Francisco, CA 91025

   b. Dates and times:

   > December 27, 1939 at 5:35 a.m.
   > It took them 3 hours, 22 minutes, and 45 seconds to cross the river.

   c. Volume, chapter, and pages numbers:

   > Chapter 10, pages 38–41
   > Vol. I, Chs 6–9

   d. Act, scene, and line numbers:

   > Act I, Scene 5, lines 7–11

   (The act is usually written with Roman numerals.)

   e. Exact amounts of money

   > $29.95   3.47 DM   25 cents apiece.

## • Abbreviations

Use commonly accepted forms of **abbreviations** or **acronyms**. Check with your dictionary if you are unsure of the correct form. You may abbreviate

1. titles before or after a name:

Capt. Kim Ferson                     Wilfred Lee Pence, Jr.
Dr. Anselm Rietdorof                 Joseph Kennedy, Sr.
Ms. Regina Carleton                  Sen. Frank Lauche

2. degrees after a name:

J. M. David, M.D.                    George Majewski, D.D.S.
Terence Wilmer, Ph.D.                B. Terry Williams, M.A.

**NOTE:** Avoid the redundancy of titles and degrees:

WRONG: Dr. Robert Speckhard, Ph.D.
RIGHT: Dr. Robert Speckhard
(or) Robert Speckhard, Ph.D.

3. time periods:

A.M.              B.C.              S.P.T.
E.S.T.            P.M.              A.D.

4. Some foreign terms:

etc. (and so forth)          et. al. (and others)
r.s.v.p. (please reply)      vs. (versus)

5. government agencies and other well-known organizations:

FBI   FDA   IRS   NATO   CARE   GE

### Misused

Do **not** abbreviate the names of states, countries, continents, months, days of the week, units of measure, college courses, and words that are part of a street or a name. Only in footnotes, bibliographies, tabulations, addresses on letters, and in personal notetaking are these sometimes abbreviated to conserve space. They are never abbreviated in narration.

WRONG: My home ec. class meets on Tues. and Thurs. through Dec.

RIGHT: My home economics class meets on Tuesday and Thursday through December.

### Spelled Out

Spell out the complete phrase or title the first time an acronym is used, placing the acronym in parentheses after it.

The non-commissioned officer (NCO) must be a model for his men and women.

# • Capitalization

Capital letters make written statements easier to read. Use capitals in accordance with established conventions. Be aware that the meaning of the word can sometimes be affected by the use of a capital, e.g., *Turkey* and *turkey*, *Catholic* and *catholic*.

1. Capitalize the first word of a sentence, including a quoted sentence. (See also Quotation Marks, p. 59.)

    John said, "*My* mind is a blank!"

2. Capitalize the first word of a line of traditional poetry.

    The woods are lovely, dark, and deep,
    But I have promises to keep,
    And miles to go before I sleep,
    And miles to go before I sleep.

    Robert Frost

**NOTE:** Many poets, however, do not prefer to capitalize according to the traditional rules.

    the greedy the people
    (as if as can yes)
    they sell and they buy
    and they die for because
    though the bell in the steeple
    says Why

    e e cummings

3. Capitalize words that are personified:

    Joy and Temperance and Repose
    Slam the door on the doctor's nose.

    Anonymous

4. Capitalize the pronoun **I**, the interjection **O**, or **OH** and most nouns and pronouns referring to the deity and terms of religious significance.

> His Word  Holy Ghost  Mother of God  Allah
> How I suffer, O Lamb of God!

5. Capitalize words referring to specific persons, places, things, times, days and months, events, organizations, ethnic groups, religions, family relationships, and words referring to heads of nations.

> Kathy Davis  College Park  Big Mac  New Year's Eve  Super Bowl
> National Organization for Women  Indian  Hindu  Uncle Freddy
> President

**NOTE:** The names of relatives are usually not capitalized. If, however, these words are used as a name of a person, they are capitalized.

> I asked my father what time he would pick me up.
> What time will you pick me up, Father?
> I need to write Mom a letter.

6. Capitalize the titles of books, plays, magazines, trade names, scientific names, newspapers, articles, poems, essays, and works of art and music.

**NOTE:** All words in the title are capitalized except conjunctions, prepositions, and the articles *a, an, the* unless these words begin the title.

> *How to Write a Term Paper*           *Death of a Salesman*
> "A Modest Proposal"                   *The New Republic*
> Mona Lisa                             *The New York Times*
> "Stopping by a Woods on a Snowy Night"
> "Two Ways of Seeing a River"

7. Capitalize geographic locations when they refer to specific areas of a country or of the world.

> West Coast  Eastern Shore  Old West

8. Capitalize words that are set off for unusual emphasis.

> Directions:
> Answer the question briefly. THINK BEFORE YOU WRITE. Support
> any assertions that you make with evidence from the text.

9. Do **not** capitalize the following:

**a.** names of seasons:

> After a long *winter*, I yearn for the greeness of *spring*.

**b.** family relationships preceded by a possessive adjective:

> My *mother* doesn't speak to Uncle Jack any longer.

**c.** common nouns mistaken for specific places or things:

> WRONG: I took Chemistry when I was still in *High School*.
> RIGHT: I took Chemistry when I was still in high school.

**d.** directions mistaken for geographic locations:

> WRONG: I drove *North* on the Bayshore Freeway.
> RIGHT: I drove north on the Bayshore Freeway.

# • Italics

**Italics** is a special, slanting type style that contrasts with the standard type normally used in printing. [In the typed or handwritten document, italics are indicated by the single underline.]

**1.** Italicize the titles of books, newspapers, periodicals, scientific names, legal cases, movies, dramas, television and radio shows, record albums, videorecordings, paintings, operas, symphonies, ships, and aircraft.

> *The World of Garp*            *Journal of New England Medicine*
> *International Herald Tribune*   *Felis catus*
> *American Bandstand*           *U.S.S. Enterprise*
> Beethoven's *Ninth Symphony*   *Air Force One*
> *Dance Hits of the 1600's*     *Plessy* v. *Ferguson*
> *The Last Supper*              *Romeo and Juliet*

**2.** Italicize letters, numbers, and words when these are referred to as entities within a sentence.

> The European *1* looks like the American *7*.
> I can't tell the difference between your *n*'s and your *u*'s.
> Don't start so many sentences with *there*, *this*, or *it*.

**3.** Italicize to add emphasis to a word, phrase or sentence.

> Mae West's famous line was "Come up and *see* me sometime, baby."
> I'm interested in *men*, not in *boys*.

**4.** Italicize foreign words and phrases that have not been assimilated into the English language.

> There are no real speed limits on the Italian *autostrada*—only suggestions.

Many foreign words have been accepted through constant use into the English language and no longer require italics.

> Why should anyone care that she chose to decorate her place in early kitsch? She's never pretended to be an expert in avant garde art.

> REMEMBER: WHEN IN DOUBT, CHECK A RELIABLE DICTIONARY

# THREE

# Common Sentence Faults

What follows is an abbreviated list of do's and don'ts covering sentence faults which can trip up the unwary writer. Such rules are—necessarily—as dry as day-old bread. You might well ask, why bother with them? To this question there are two answers—one of them is perhaps obvious, the other less so.

Most grammar rules are there to assure communication. By following them, we keep our message to the reader clear and avoid confusion and misunderstanding. Since communication is our primary goal, it makes sense to eliminate grammatical static.

But other grammar rules (not as many) are simply conventional and arbitrary. If we break them, our reader will still get our message. However, that same reader may notice the broken rule and then make some unwanted assumptions about us as writers. Unfortunately and perhaps unfairly, people often judge us by the way we use or misuse language. Reports are rejected, job applications are turned down, promotions are denied simply because "whoever wrote that doesn't know proper English." In other words, when we break the rules, we run the risk of irritating our readers, distracting them from what we want to say and having them criticize us for the way we said it. To command their attention and their respect, we need to learn the rules.

# Problems with Sentence Structure •

## • Fragments

As we know from Chapter One, a sentence must include both a subject and predicate, and it must express a complete thought. (Note: a full understanding of a sentence's meaning may depend on its context, but structurally it should stand on its own.)

A fragment is a pseudo-sentence, a group of words which the writer has punctuated like a sentence (capitalizing the first letter, putting a period at the end), but which fails to meet one or more of the three requirements. When we read such a fragment, we feel that something is missing. The writer has left us in suspense.

### 1. Missing Subjects, Missing Verbs

Many fragments occur in the middle of a paragraph. Often the writer has felt that a subject or verb from one sentence can carry over to the next, that it can be "understood" or "implied."

> I'd really like to go out tonight. Either to a movie or to the basketball game.

But grammar does not allow this kind of borrowing. The fragment must either be incorporated into the preceding "legal" sentence or be given its own subject and verb.

> I'd really like to go out tonight, either to a movie or to the basketball game.

or

> I'd really like to go out tonight. We could go either to a movie or to the basketball game.

### 2. Verbs vs. Verbals

A sentence predicate must include a complete verb. Verbals (participles, gerunds, and infinitives) do not meet this requirement.

> The boys were busy all afternoon. *Making* sandwiches and packing their cooler with beer before the concert.
> After dieting for three weeks, he was pleased when he weighed himself. *To discover* that he had lost five pounds.
> Susan likes all kinds of sports, including volleyball, soccer and tennis. *Swimming* and *jogging* too.

To correct a fragment of this kind, the writer must either attach the verbal phrase to an appropriate sentence or supply a complete subject and verb.

> The boys were busy all afternoon making sandwiches and packing their cooler with beer before the concert.
> After dieting for three weeks, he was pleased when he weighed himself to discover that he had lost five pounds.

or

> After dieting for three weeks, he was pleased when he weighed himself. He discovered that he had lost five pounds.
> Susan likes all kinds of sports, including volleyball, soccer and tennis. She likes swimming and jogging too.

## 3. Subordinate Clauses

A fragment of this kind contains the necessary subject and predicate, but the clause as a whole depends for its meaning on another clause; by itself, it does not express a complete thought. Dependent or subordinate clauses can be recognized because they begin with words such as *although, because, when, if, until, who, which*—these words all suggest a necessary connection linking the clause that follows them to some other thought. (See Chapter One, p. 33 on subordinate conjunctions and relative pronouns.)

> Taking evening classes hasn't been easy for me. Since I have to leave work early to get to school on time.

Once again, such a fragment usually belongs to another nearby sentence and should be attached to it.

> Taking evening classes hasn't been easy for me, since I have to leave work early to get to school on time.

Alternatively, the fragment may be rewritten as an independent clause, minus its subordinate conjunction or relative pronoun.

> Taking evening classes hasn't been easy for me. *I have* to leave work early to get to school on time.

### A final note on fragments:

Despite all these warnings and the wrath of countless English teachers, fragments abound. We see them every day in advertisements, in newspaper headlines, in memos and letters, in records of spoken dialogue. Experienced writers use fragments deliberately to enhance descriptive passages or to add an idiomatic flair to their prose. In university assignments, however, and in other formal writing situations, you are safest sticking to complete sentences. Leave the fragments to the journalists and novelists.

# • Run-on Sentences

This problem is the flip side or opposite of the sentence fragment.

> A soldier may get orders from two different people it's hard to know which order to follow.

Here the writer has punctuated two structurally complete sentences as if they were one. The reader, expecting one complete thought, is confronted with two and must back-track over the sentence to separate them.

You might think that a simple comma inserted in the right place would solve the problem. Certainly it is better than nothing, but by itself a comma is not sufficient to fix a run-on sentence. To do a proper job, four solutions are possible:

1. Separate the two clauses by a period. In other words, make two sentences.

> A soldier may get orders from two different people. It's hard to know which order to follow.

2. Separate the two clauses by a semicolon. This is useful if the ideas contained in the two clauses are in fact closely related.

> A soldier may get orders from two different people; it's hard to know which order to follow.

3. Link the two clauses by an appropriate coordinating conjunction such as *and*, *but*, or *so*. Be sure to place a comma before the conjunction so that the reader can see where one clause ends and another begins.

> A soldier may get orders from two different people, *and* it's hard to know which order to follow.

4. Change one of the clauses to a subordinate clause by adding an appropriate subordinating conjunction or relative pronoun. Be sure to link the two clauses together. This solution also helps to clarify the relationship between the two ideas being presented.

> *If* a soldier gets orders from two different people, it's hard to know which order to follow.

COMMON SENTENCE FAULTS

**NOTE:** Writers often fall into the run-on trap when they begin a second main clause with *therefore, however, then, for example* or similar transitional words. (They will insert a comma but still have a run-on sentence.) These transitional words are *not* coordinating conjunctions and thus cannot link main clauses. Treat them strictly as adverbs that show relationships between clauses.

WRONG

I borrowed a couple of videotapes from my neighbor, however they turned out to be really boring.
I took the tapes back, then I went out to visit some friends.

In this case, solution #2 using a semi-colon is usually best. Notice that the semi-colon is inserted *before* the transitional word. Also, unless a transitional word is very short, a comma is inserted *following* it. (See Chapter Two, pp. 43.)

RIGHT

I borrowed a couple of videotapes from my neighbor; however, they turned out to be really boring.
I took the tapes back; then I went out to visit some friends.

## • Awkward Sentences

In addition to being structurally complete units, sentences should make sense logically. This seems an elementary rule, but in the heat of composition or the rush to meet a deadline, a writer will often start a sentence in one mode and finish it in another, with confusing results for the reader.

In Hemingway's story it tells about a man and his wife on a safari in Africa.

(The *story* tells about the man and his wife, so why is *it* the subject of the sentence?)

The applause inspired the singer had confidence and seemed to perform even better.

(*Singer* is simultaneously the object of *inspired* and the subject of *had*.)

When reading over your own work, run the following checks to avoid awkward constructions:

**1.** Make sure that your subjects, verbs, and complements are logically compatible.

Hemingway's story tells about a man and his wife on a safari in Africa.

or

In his story, Hemingway tells about a man and his wife on a safari in Africa.

After the applause, the singer had confidence and seemed to perform even better.

or

The applause inspired confidence in the singer, who seemed to perform even better.

2. Keep the core elements of your clause together, unless you have special reasons for separating them. In general, readers expect to see the verb following directly after the subject, and the object or complement following the verb. Don't disappoint these expectations by inserting lengthy phrases or subordinate clauses between related elements.

AWKWARD: My boss, though she didn't look too happy about the idea, let us go home early because of the snowstorm.

COHERENT: My boss let us go home early because of the snowstorm, though she didn't look too happy about the idea.

COHERENT: Though she didn't look too happy about the idea, my boss let us go home early because of the snowstorm.

AWKWARD: Finally I managed, after trying all semester, to get a B on one of the weekly essays.

COHERENT: Finally, after trying all semester, I managed to get a B on one of the weekly essays.

# Problems with Nouns and Pronouns •

As you know from Chapter One, the function of pronouns is to substitute for other terms. Pronouns are useful to you, the writer, because they allow you to avoid boring repetition of nouns and noun phrases. But your reader needs to know what term is being substituted. In addition to this basic principle of pronoun **reference**, the reader will have expectations concerning pronoun-antecedent **agreement**, pronoun **case** and consistency in pronoun **person** and **number**.

## • Pronoun Reference

A pronoun must always refer clearly to its antecedent noun or pronoun. This basic principle leads to several important rules:

COMMON SENTENCE FAULTS

1. Make sure that each pronoun has an **explicit** antecedent. One which is implied or which modifies another term will not give sufficient identity to the pronoun.

> IMPLIED: After sanding the chair legs, she turned it upright and began varnishing.

(Here *chair* serves as an adjective modifying *legs*; thus it cannot be the antecedent for *it*.)

> EXPLICIT: After sanding the legs of the chair, she turned it upright and began varnishing.

2. Use a pronoun soon after its antecedent. If the two terms are separated by more than a sentence or two, they may fail to connect in the reader's mind.

> Colleen's surprise party was a great success. Many of her friends came, including some she hadn't seen for years. They brought funny birthday cards and thoughtful presents, reminding her of the good times they had shared. She would remember it in the months ahead.

(*It* in the last sentence refers to *party* in the first, but the antecedent is too distant to be immediately obvious. A simple solution is to replace *it* with *the party* or *the event*.)

3. Make sure that each pronoun refers clearly to a **single** antecedent. If several nouns compete for the honor, ambiguity will result.

> CONFUSING: After Bob visited Juan, he felt better.

(Who felt better?)

> CLEAR: Bob felt better after visiting Juan.
> CLEAR: After Bob's visit, Juan felt better.

> CONFUSING: Separate the egg white from the yolk. Add it to the flour.
> CLEAR: Add the yolk to the flour after separating it from the egg white.

4. Restrict your antecedents to nouns or noun phrases, not complete clauses or statements. Be particularly careful when using the pronouns *which*, *this*, *that* and *it*.

> CONFUSING: Many of the students were nervous about writing, but this did not surprise their teacher.

CHAPTER THREE

CLEAR: Many of the students were nervous about writing, but their anxiety did not surprise the teacher.

CONFUSING: The classroom was clean and well-lighted, which pleased the students.
CLEAR: The students were pleased that the classroom was clean and well-lighted.

# • Pronoun Agreement

Pronouns should "agree" with their antecedents in both number and gender. In other words, if the antecedent is singular and feminine (*daughter*), the following pronoun must also be singular and feminine (*she, her*). If the antecedent is plural (*horses*), the pronoun must be too (*they, them*). (Note that only singular pronouns indicate gender.) In most cases, simple logic will supply the proper pronoun for a given antecedent:

The company pays *its* employees well.
When the singers walked on the stage, *they* were greeted by wild applause from *their* fans.

In a few cases, however, logic and language part company. The following rules should help you choose the right pronoun in these special situations.

## 1. Collective Nouns

When your antecedent is a collective noun (*class, committee, team, army, audience*, etc.; see Chapter One, p. 4), choose either a singular *or* a plural pronoun—whichever makes most sense in the context—and use it consistently.

When the class finished *their* exam, *they* were tired.
(Plural pronouns produce consistent and logical sentence.)

When the class finished *its* exam, *they* were tired.
(Pronouns are inconsistent.)

When the class finished *its* exam, *it* was tired.
(Singular pronouns sound less logical.)

**NOTE:** You may also have to choose between a singular and plural *verb* when using a collective noun; all three terms must then agree. (See below, **Problems with Verbs**, p. 86.)

## 2. Indefinite Pronouns

Be alert to agreement problems caused by the so-called indefinite pronouns (*everyone, nobody, each*, etc.; see Chapter One, p. 23) when used as antecedents. Some of these words are plural in meaning but singular in form. Notice that they also require singular verbs. (See below, p. 85.)

*Everyone* is going to the movies tonight.

Which pronoun should be used in this context?

Everyone has bought *his*? *her*? *their*? ticket(s) ahead of time.

Several answers are possible to solve this problem:

**a.** Informal spoken English allows us to use the plural *their*, ignoring the discrepancy with the singular verb *has bought*. This solution is increasingly common in written English as well but is still rejected by most grammarians and university teachers.

**b.** Traditional grammar rules insist on the masculine singular *his*, ignoring the argument that *everyone* might include women or girls. (In this case, the pronoun is considered not masculine, but generic.) Many women, however, find this solution offensive.

In a sentence about going to the movies, the gender problem may seem trivial. But consider the following instructions for a job application:

All candidates must be interviewed. Everyone should bring *his* completed application form to the interview.

Can women apply for this job? Will they?

**c.** By using both gender pronouns (*his or her* ticket) you can satisfy the grammarians and avoid inadvertent sexism, but this solution quickly becomes very clumsy and irritating. Try reading the following:

Each applicant should bring *his or her* application form to *his or her* interview. *He or she* will also take a half-hour exam evaluating *his or her* writing skills . . .

**d.** Why not eliminate the troublesome indefinite pronoun altogether? In most cases, by rephrasing your sentence in the plural, you can avoid all of the problems encountered in **a**, **b**, and **c**. You may have to exercise your imagination.

All the movie-goers have bought *their* tickets ahead of time.

Applicants should bring *their* application forms to the interview. *They* will also take a half-hour exam evaluating *their* writing skills.

# • Pronoun Choices—Pronoun Shifts

Different writing situations demand different pronoun choices or *viewpoints*. A personal narrative may call for the first person:

"As *I* entered the room . . ."

A set of instructions may suggest the second person:

Opening the box, *you* will find three envelopes; open the blue one first.

And technical reports generally prefer the third person:

*one, he, she, it, they.*

Whichever your choice as a writer, you must keep your viewpoint consistent and appropriate to the given solution. Hence the following rules:

1. Avoid arbitrary shifts from one pronoun to another:

   *One* needs to jot down necessary items ahead of time if *you* expect to shop efficiently.
   (Third person shifts to second person.)

   A dog must learn to obey *its* owner; otherwise, *they* become a nuisance.
   (Singular shifts to plural.)

   Whenever *I* have to give a speech, *I* practice in front of a mirror; that way *you* don't get stage fright.
   (First person shifts to second person.)

2. When using the "you" viewpoint, make sure that the second-person pronoun is appropriate to the situation. Are you in fact addressing the reader? If not, substitute a more accurate pronoun.

   INAPPROPRIATE: In Classical Greece (as in the 20th century), *you* could make a name for *yourself* by winning in the Olympic Games.

   APPROPRIATE: In Classical Greece, *athletes* could make names for *themselves* by winning in the Olympic Games.

**NOTE:** The use of "you" is only rarely appropriate in formal writing.

COMMON SENTENCE FAULTS

# • Pronoun Case

Pronouns, unlike nouns, change form according to their use in a sentence; thus we speak of the **subjective case**, the **objective case** and the **possessive case**. (See Chapter One, p. 5.) (Nouns show a possessive case by the use of an apostrophe, as we saw in Chapter Two.)

In simple sentences, we will usually choose the right pronoun case without hesitation:

*I* went swimming this morning
(not *Me* went swimming.)

But in more complex structures, the choice isn't always so obvious, and you may need to refer to the following rules:

1. In compound subjects, be sure to use subjective pronouns.

   At the picnic, Gary and *I* (not *me*) shared our ice cream with a stray bulldog.
   After the concert, *she* (not *her*) and her brother took a walk.

NOTE: If in doubt, try out the pronoun alone to see if it sounds right. (*She* took a walk.)

2. In the same way, use objective case pronouns in compound object constructions (direct objects, indirect objects, objects of a preposition).

   The newspaper criticized both *him* (not *he*) and the other players for their remarks. (direct object)
   The secretary gave Rudy and *her* (not *she*) the information they needed. (indirect object)
   There is only one problem between you and *me* (not *I*)—we can never stop arguing. (object of a preposition)

3. Be particularly careful when using the relative/interrogative pronouns *who*, *whom* and *which*.

   a. Use *who* and *whom* (not *which*) to refer to people.

      I spoke with the technician *who* had developed the new procedure.
      I can't remember the singer for *whom* that song was composed.

   b. Use *who* when a subjective case is required; use *whom* when the sentence calls for an objective case.

CHAPTER THREE

Fred wanted to know *who* had been chosen to be the new publicity director. (subject of subordinate clause)
For *whom* did you buy Christmas presents this year? (object of preposition)
*Whom* are you inviting to your party? (direct object)

**NOTE:** Since these pronouns are often misused in informal speech and writing, the correct case may sound odd or stuffy. If so, avoid the whole problem by rephrasing your sentence another way.

Fred wanted to know the election results for the new publicity director.
Who was on your Christmas shopping list this year?
Who is coming to your party?

If in doubt whether a subjective or objective pronoun is required, try substituting the corresponding personal pronoun:

*She* (not *her*) had been chosen to be the new publicity director.
(hence, *who*, not *whom*)
Did you buy Christmas presents for *them* (not *they*) this year? (hence *whom*, not *who*).

4. When using a pronoun after *than* or *as*, determine the proper pronoun case by mentally completing your intended comparison.

David likes Paolo better than I.
(Here you mean: better than I do.)

David likes Paolo better than me.
(Here you mean: better than David likes me.)

**NOTE:** To save your reader the same doubts you went through concerning the proper pronoun, it is often better simply to supply the missing verb or phrase.

She is a better student than *he*? than *him*?
She is a better student than *he is*. (subject of verb *is*)

The other team just doesn't work as hard as *they*? as *them*?
The other team just doesn't work as hard as *they do*.

# Problems with Verbs •

Because they carry so much of the meaning in a sentence, verbs attract the reader's attention. Well-chosen active verbs can give your writing real punch; conversely, errors in using verbs can cripple an otherwise effective sentence.

Several potential verb problems have already received attention in this book. Irregular verbs often trip up the writer with their unexpected past tense or participle forms (see Chapter One, p. 7); participles masquerading as complete predicates can lead to sentence fragments (see above, p. 72). The rules which follow cover other aspects of verb use you will need to master.

## • Subject-Verb Agreement

Just as pronouns must agree with their antecedents, verbs must agree with their subjects in number. Singular subjects require singular verbs; plural subjects demand plural verbs. For many sentences, this rule is easily applied, either because the subject-verb combination is simple and straightforward (*We like* this pizza place.) or because the verb is in the past or future tense, in which the singular and plural forms are identical.

> *He ran* to the phone.          *She will accept* the job.
> *They ran* to the phone.        *They will accept* the job.

In practical terms, we need to make "agreement" choices only when writing in the present tense:

> The *hamburger tastes* good.
> The *french fries taste* even better.

or when using forms of the auxiliary verbs *to be* or *to have*:

> *He was working* late last night.      *It has disappeared.*
> *They were working* late last night.   *They have disappeared.*

Keep in mind the following rules of verb-subject agreement:

1. Be sure the verb agrees with the subject, even if they are separated by other intervening words or phrases. Don't be misled by prepositional or verbal phrases which often follow immediately after the subject.

> verbal phrase
>
> The *road* connecting the two towns *follows* the river.

prepositional phrases

The *flowers* in the glass vase on the table *were* already *drooping* in the heat.

**NOTE:** A singular subject followed by words such as *together with*, *including*, *in addition to*, or *as well as* remains singular.

George as well as Angie *is coming* to the seminar.

Since such sentences often sound awkward, it is usually best to rewrite them.

George and Angie are both *coming* to the seminar.

**2.** Two subjects joined by *and* will always take a plural verb. This makes sense since you are basically adding the two together. (See compound subject, p. 11.)

The *computer* and the *printer take* up a lot of space on my desk.

**3.** When two subjects are joined by *or*, the verb should agree with the subject nearest to it. Here you are no longer "adding" the two subjects, but "choosing" between them.

Either the *earrings* or the *necklace was* on sale.

In sentences like these, a plural verb will sound more natural, so if one of your subjects is plural, put it closest to the verb.

Either the *necklace* or the *earrings were* on sale.

**4.** Make sure that a linking verb (such as *is*, *seems*, *becomes*) agrees with the subject and *not* with the complement which follows the verb.

Her one real *enthusiasm is* her canaries.

Again, you can rearrange such a sentence to allow a more natural-sounding plural verb.

*Canaries are* her one real enthusiasm.

**5.** When the subject follows the verb, be especially careful. The verb must still agree. Word order may be inverted

**a.** with the expletives *here* or *there*:

COMMON SENTENCE FAULTS

> Here *comes* the *bus* we've been waiting for.
> There *were* two *sets* of keys on the table.
> Well, there *go* our *profits.*

**b.** in descriptive or emphatic sentences:

> Over the rolling seas *hang* menacing *stormclouds.*
> We've been waiting for an hour, and now in *walk Dan and Jennie.*

**c.** in interrogative sentences, especially those beginning with *when,* *where* or *why*:

> Where *are* the *hammer* and *nails* you promised to bring me?

6. In subordinate clauses beginning with the relative pronouns *who, which* or *that*, the verb must agree with the antecedent in the main clause.

> She always buys furniture from stores *that offer* home delivery.
> (Antecedent is plural *stores.*)

> He is probably the only one of the students *who likes* to take tests.
> (The word *only* gives you the singular context to identify *one* as the antecedent.)

> Fitzsimmons is one of those teachers *who demand* hard work from their students.
> (Antecedent is *teachers*, not *one*. Fitzsimmons belongs to a group of teachers, all of whom expect hard work.)

7. When using indefinite pronouns as subjects, be alert to potential problems in verb agreement. (These words cause headaches when used as antecedents too—see above, p. 79.)

**a.** The following pronouns ending in *-one, -body*, and *-thing* require singular verbs:

| | | |
|---|---|---|
| *one* | *everyone* | *nothing* |
| *no one* | *nobody* | *anything* |
| *anyone* | *anybody* | *something* |
| *someone* | *somebody* | *everything* |
| | *everybody* | |

> *Somebody was knocking* at the door, but *no one* in the room *was* willing to open it.

CHAPTER THREE

In addition, the pronouns *each*, *either*, *neither* and *another* also take singular verbs.

> *Each* of us *takes* a chance whenever we get behind the wheel.
> *Neither* of the teams *was* willing to accept defeat.

**b.** The pronoun *both* always takes a plural verb.

> *Both* of you *deserve* a bonus.

**c.** The pronouns *none*, *any*, *some*, *more*, *most* and *all* may take either a singular or a plural verb. The choice depends on the noun they refer to.

> I'd like a piece of cake. *Is* there *any* left?
> (*Any* refers to *cake*.)

> I'd prefer a cookie or two. There *are some* on the plate.
> (*Some* refers to implied *cookies*.)

> *Most* of the books *have* already *been checked* out.
> *None* of the students *like* that course.
> *None* of the food *was* left after the party.

**8.** Collective nouns (see also above, p. 78) are usually considered as units and thus take singular verbs.

> The *army has expanded* in recent years.
> The *majority has voted* in favor of the proposal.

However, such sentences may prove awkward, especially if the context includes subsequent pronouns which must also agree with the collective noun.

> Each time the singer reappears, the *audience claps its* hands enthusiastically.
> (The audience appears to have one giant set of hands.)

In a case like this, you may want to use a plural verb and pronoun or—better still—rewrite the sentence to avoid agreement problems.

> Each time the singer reappears, the *listeners clap their* hands enthusiastically.

> Each time the singer reappears, the *audience applauds* enthusiastically.

**9.** A number of words and phrases may have a plural appearance but a singular meaning. As subjects they require singular verbs.

    **a.** Titles of books, movies, etc.

> *Star Wars was* a box-office smash.

    **b.** Subjects indicating quantity, when considered as a unit—such as distances, measurements, sums of money, etc.

> *Twenty-two kilometers is* equal to ten miles.
> I still think that *thirty dollars is* a lot to pay for a pair of sandals.

**NOTE:** If the items making up the quantity are considered as separate parts, the verb may be plural.

> Only *one third* of the students *have turned* in their papers.

    **c.** A small group of nouns which end in -s and look plural but are considered to have a singular meaning: news, mathematics, physics, ethics, politics, economics, athletics, etc.

> *Politics is* a fascinating spectator sport, but more people need to participate—by voting.

## • Shifts in Tense, Voice, and Mood

Just as readers expect agreement between subject and verb, they also count on a consistent use of verbs, both within the individual sentence and from one sentence to the next. It is disconcerting when a writer begins in the present tense and then shifts unnecessarily into the past or when one clause proceeds in the active voice and the next shifts to the passive. You can achieve consistency in verb use by following simple rules.

**1.** Avoid arbitrary shifts in tense. Unless your meaning requires a change, choose an appropriate tense and stick with it throughout a sentence or passage.

> INCONSISTENT:    When the movie *begins*, we *saw* the hero in training camp; later he *was flying* an F-16 in a dogfight; but at the end he *gets* shot down and *dies*.

CHAPTER THREE

| | |
|---|---|
| CONSISTENT PRESENT TENSE: | When the movie *begins*, we *see* the hero in training camp; later he *is flying* an F-16 in a dogfight; but at the end he *gets* shot down and *dies*. |
| CONSISTENT PAST TENSE: | When the movie *began*, we *saw* the hero in training camp; later he *was flying* an F-16 in a dogfight; but at the end he *got* shot down and *died*. |

**2.** When choosing tenses, use the sequence that accurately reflects the chronology of actions described.

| | |
|---|---|
| CONFUSING: | She *was* away from home for six months when she *received* word that her grandmother *has* died. |
| ACCURATE: | She *had* been away from home for six months when she *received* word that her grandmother *had* died. |

(Past perfect tense is used to indicate events occurring previous to an event related in past tense.)

| | |
|---|---|
| CONFUSING: | Next year *I'm looking* for a new job, but for now *I'll hold* on to the one *I have* for the past five years. |
| ACCURATE: | Next year *I'll look* for a new job, but for now *I'm holding on* to the one *I've had* for the past five years. |

**3.** Use the present tense in the following situations:

**a.** when asserting general truths or accepted facts.

> She reminded him that *carrots are* a good source of vitamin A.
> As a rule, *students detest* grammar books like this one.

**b.** when describing habitual actions.

> *I wash* the dog every three months or so.

**c.** in critical writing about literature and other arts.

> Leonardo da Vinci's understanding of aeronautics *is* really amazing; his notebooks *show* detailed drawings of various flying machines.

**4.** Use active voice verbs both to convey information efficiently and to give your writing greater energy.

Read the following news story, first in the passive voice and then in the active:

A daring raid was made on the Westland Bank on Main Street at 10 o'clock this morning by a gang of men with stockings over their heads. The incident was described by Mr. Ronald Smith, 55, a clerk at the bank. The staff was forced to lie on the floor while the safe was opened; $50,000 in used bank notes and jewelry worth $30,000 were stolen. The robbery was carried out by five men, all carrying guns.

At 10 o'clock this morning a gang of men with stockings over their heads daringly raided the Westland Bank of Main Street. Mr. Ronald Smith, 55, a clerk at the bank, described the incident. The robbers forced the staff to lie on the floor while they opened the safe, stealing $50,000 in used bank notes and jewelry worth $30,000. Five men, all carrying guns, carried out the robbery.

**5.** Use passive voice verbs only when what happens is more important than who or what makes it happen—or when you don't know who or what is responsible.

> Good news—I've *been promoted*!
> Telephone service *was restored* 48 hours after the storm.
> His car *was stolen* from the parking lot last night.

**6.** When giving directions or instructions, use either the imperative (command) mood or the indicative, not both. (See Chapter One, p. 10.)

SHIFT IN MOOD: To make the pancakes, *combine* the dry ingredients and then *you should add* the milk and eggs.

(*combine* is imperative, *you should add* is indicative)

CONSISTENT MOOD: To make the pancakes, *combine* the dry ingredients and then *add* the milk and eggs.

# • Missing Verb Parts

Tenses other than the simple past and present require auxiliary verbs to complete the meaning of the main verb. (See Chapter One, p. 8.)

**1.** Remember that participles require helping verbs in order to function as complete predicates. (Though not observed in some American dialects, this rule is inviolable in standard English.)

NOT: Sociologists *seen* what the population explosion *done* to traditional family structure.

BUT: Sociologists *have seen* what the population explosion *has done* to traditional family structure.

**2.** When using compound verbs of different tenses, be sure to include all the verb parts needed for each tense.

> INCOMPLETE:   I always have and always will believe in freedom of the press.

(Present perfect tense requires *believed* not *believe*.)

> COMPLETE:   I always have believed and always will believe in freedom of the press.

**NOTE:**   Such sentences often end up sounding self-consciously correct or even pompous. It's usually best to reword them.

> I have always been a firm believer in freedom of the press and always will be.

# Problems with Modifiers •

Modifiers allow us to make our sentences more precise and more interesting. Instead of simple stating "Joanne wrote an essay," we can sketch in a few details:

> Pressed for time, Joanne quickly wrote a 300-word descriptive essay.

Or we can use adjectives, adverbs, participles, infinitives, and prepositional phrases to describe Joanne's plight in graphic detail:

> Hunched over her tiny desk for two frantic hours, Joanne wrote furiously, crumpling page after blotted page into the wastebasket but finally cranking out—just in time for class—300 forgettable words describing in minute and boring detail her summer vacation job as an elevator operator.

Now the interesting fact about this last enormous sentence is that it is still readable. So long as we choose appropriate modifying words or phrases and keep them clearly attached to their respective nouns or verbs, we can lead our readers through a labyrinth of even 50 or 60 words. (Our sample sentence had 46.)

But to use modifiers effectively, even in short sentences, we need to keep in mind a number of basic guidelines.

COMMON SENTENCE FAULTS

# •  Adjectives and Adverbs: Right Choices, Right Forms

1. Use adverbs, not adjectives, to modify verbs, adjectives, or other adverbs.

| MODIFYING VERBS: | He learns *quickly*. (not *quick*)<br>She *surely* knows how to cook. (not *sure*)<br>They won the game *easily*. (not *easy*) |
|---|---|
| MODIFYING OTHER ADVERBS: | Today she arrived *unusually* early for work. (not *unusual*)<br>My new car is *considerably* more efficient than my old one. (not *considerable*) |
| MODIFYING ADJECTIVES: | I'm *terribly* sorry about the missed appointment. (not *terrible*)<br>That was a *really* wretched movie. (not *real*) |

The adjective and adverb forms are identical for a few words such as *fast, hard, early, straight*.

The F-20 is a *fast* plane.
Georgio types *fast*.

But these are the exceptions. In most cases, you will need to distinguish carefully between adjective and adverb forms. Check the dictionary if in doubt.

2. Following linking verbs (like *be, seem, appear, become*) and verbs describing the senses (like *feel, see, taste, smell*), choose either an adjective or an adverb, depending on what your modifier is modifying. Use an adjective to modify the subject; use an adverb to modify the verb.

The lion looked *calmly* at the spectators.

They looked *calm* to him.

Without my glasses on, I see quite *badly*.

I like watching that woman play softball. She is *good*.

This okra casserole tastes *terrible*.

**NOTE:** In referring to someone's health, use the modifiers *well* and *bad*, not *good* and *badly*.

CHAPTER THREE

After yesterday's attack of food poisoning, I felt really *bad*, but today I feel quite *well*.

3. In general, avoid using nouns to modify other nouns; use an appropriate adjective instead. Compare the following:

| | | |
|---|---|---|
| management goals | vs. | managerial goals |
| dependence variables | vs. | dependent variables |
| education opportunities | vs. | educational opportunities |

Long strings of multisyllabic abstract nouns are a trademark of bureaucratic prose (*merit equity objectives*, *contingency authorization availability*, etc.); their effect—and sometimes their purpose—is to baffle the reader. Try to avoid such phrases. (See Chapter One, p. 21.)

4. For both adjectives and adverbs, use the positive, comparative and superlative forms appropriately. (See Chapter One, p. 25.)

Note that some adjectives have no comparative or superlative forms; they are "absolute." Either something is *perfect* or it is not; it cannot be *more perfect* or *most perfect*. *Infinite*, *unique*, *impossible* and *pregnant* are also absolute, as are *round*, *square* and other such geometrical terms. To establish gradations, we must use adverbial modifiers:

His discovery had *nearly infinite* possibilities.
The answer given was *somewhat less than perfect*.

5. Demonstrative adjectives (*this*, *that*, *these*, *those*) serve to specify particular nouns and pronouns, distinguishing them from others of the same class.

SPECIFIC: Do you see *those* two cars over there? I just saw them run three stoplights.
*This* is the taco sauce I prefer.
*That* one is made for fire-eating dragons.

Used without such specific reference, these demonstrative adjectives will only fog your writing with vague generalities.

VAGUE: He woke up feeling *those* Monday-morning blues. (*which ones?*)
SPECIFIC: He woke up feeling the Monday-morning blues: five bleak working days lay between now and next weekend's party.

# • Placement: Putting Modifiers Where They Belong

1. Position adverbs close to the word or phrase they are modifying. Our tendency in spoken English is to put them right before the verb, but this is not always appropriate.

> MISLEADING: She *almost* ran a mile to get help.
> CLEAR:      She ran *almost* a mile to get help.

a. Be especially careful when using the common adverbs *only, hardly, almost, just, nearly* and *even*. These adverbs can sometimes alter the meaning of a sentence simply by shifting position.

> *Just* last weekend I realized I had enough money in the bank to buy a VCR.
> Last weekend I realized I had *just* enough money in the bank to buy a VCR.
> Last weekend I realized I had enough money *just* in the bank to buy a VCR.

> The two companies *nearly* went broke after completing the merger.
> The two companies went broke after *nearly* completing the merger.

Although you will not always notice such obvious changes in meaning, you will achieve greater clarity by putting your adverbs where they belong.

b. Avoid placing a modifier between two phrases, both of which it might logically refer to. It will then be ambiguous, suggesting two quite different meanings.

> Joe promised me *today* he would finish the job.

This sentence could mean that Joe *made the promise today* or that he contracted to *finish the job today*. The reader has no way of knowing what the writer meant to say. You could rewrite the sentence several ways:

> Today Joe promised me he would finish the job.
> Joe promised me he would finish the job today.
> Joe promised me today that he would finish the job.

(For use of the subordinating conjunction *that*, see below, p. 99.)

2. Remember that phrases and clauses acting as adjectives or adverbs should also refer clearly to the words they modify.

   a. Put a phrase or clause used as an adjective near the noun it modifies. Otherwise, it may "attach" itself to the closest available noun— sometimes with surprising changes in meaning.

      The Senate approved the spending bill for the new missiles *with strings attached.*
      (Now what has the strings attached?)

      The store clerk recommended a reinforced leash for my new dog *that is practically indestructible.*
      (quite a dog!)

   Sometimes such phrases are clear if placed at the beginning or end of the sentence.

      *When blinking,* the stoplight requires motorists to slow down.

   But occasionally this solution creates confusion.

      The stoplight requires motorists to slow down *when blinking.*
      (only when the *motorists* are blinking?)

   Of course, you as the writer know what you mean, but will the innocent readers? Read through your sentences from their point of view.

   b. Adverb phrases and clauses are more flexible in their position, but you can avoid potential ambiguity by placing them near the verb, adjective or adverb they are modifying. Compare the following sentences:

      *Before I left town* I decided to stop at the next gas station.

      (I *made the decision* before leaving town.)

      I decided to stop at the next gas station *before I left town.*

      (I decided *to stop* before leaving town.)

3. Be sure that your adjective modifiers, such as participle phrases, always have an appropriate noun or pronoun to modify; this noun or pronoun must be explicit, not merely implied in the sentence. Without something to modify, the adjective will "dangle."

COMMON SENTENCE FAULTS

> DANGLING:  Having survived the shipwreck, his one hope was to
>               reach the lifeboat.

(Who survived the shipwreck? He did, of course. But "he" isn't in the sentence.)

> CLEAR:      Having survived the shipwreck, he had only one
>               hope—to reach the lifeboat.

a.  Remember that introductory verbal phrases (those which begin the sentence) must modify the subject of the sentence.

> DANGLING:  *If lost*, the airline's baggage claim office will assume
>               responsibility.

(*Baggage claim office* is the subject.)

> DANGLING:  *When packing for a camping trip*, check lists are
>               advisable.

(*Check lists* is the subject.)

Often the best solution for such a dangling modifier is to expand it into a full clause, so that the verbal will have its own subject.

> If your suitcase is lost, the airline's baggage claim office will assume
> responsibility.
> When one is packing for a camping trip, check lists are advisable.

b.  Take care with so-called "elliptical" clauses (shortened versions in which subject and verb are implied but not spelled out); they too must clearly modify an explicit noun or pronoun.

> DANGLING:  *When in the army*, the rules have to be followed—or
>               else.

Again you can fix such a dangling clause by filling in its missing subject and verb or by rewriting the main clause.

> When a person is in the army, the rules have to be followed—or
> else.
> When in the army, a soldier must follow the rules—or else.

## • Agreement

Most adjectives do not have differing singular and plural forms and thus will automatically "agree" with whatever noun they modify.

There *I* sat, *fat, dumb, and happy.*
There *we* sat, *fat, dumb, and happy.*

1. One exception to this rule is the group of possessive adjectives (*my, our, her, their*, etc.) which must agree with their antecedent, not with the noun following them.

   Don't tell me it's *my* mistake when it's *your* mistake.

2. A second exception is the set of demonstrative adjectives *this, that, these,* and *those*. This second group can cause agreement problems when used to modify the phrases *type of, sort of, kind of, make of, brand of*. In spoken English we often hear a sentence such as the following:

   *These sort* of engines are very powerful.

   Yet the subject of the sentence is singular: *sort*. To show proper agreement, the sentence should therefore read

   *This* sort of engine *is* very powerful.
   (Both the adjective and the verb must be singular.)

   If, instead, the writer intends to discuss several varieties of engines, the sentence will read

   *These* sorts of engines *are* very powerful.
   (Adjective and verb are plural.)

   In most cases, however, the *sort of* or *type of* phrase is really superfluous, adding nothing to the meaning of the sentence. We can rewrite the sentence without it—and save ourselves the headache of matching appropriate adjectives and verbs.

   This engine is very powerful.
   These engines are very powerful.

**NOTE:** If you do use these phrases, remember to include the *of*.

COMMON SENTENCE FAULTS

NOT:  That type armchair is on sale.
BUT:  That type *of* armchair is on sale.

## Articles

The articles *a*, *an* and *the* constitute a tiny subgroup of the adjective family. (See Chapter One, p. 23.) Since there are only three of them in the whole language, you wouldn't think they could cause many problems. Nor will they, if you keep in mind the following points:

1.  Choose between *a* and *an* according to the opening sound of the word which follows the article. *A* precedes consonant sounds, while *an* precedes vowel sounds.

    *a* disaster, *a* zipper, *a* beautiful day, *a* unicorn
    (Although unicorn starts with a vowel, its initial sound is a **y**, as in *you*.)

    When a word begins with **u**, listen to it:
    *a* useful fact, *an* unlikely alibi

    *an* isolated post, *an* overdose, *an* idiotic remark, *an* hour
    (Although *hour* begins with a consonant, its initial sound is **ow** or **ou**, as in *ouch*!)

    When a word begins with *h*, listen to it:
    *an* honor, *a* happening

2.  Remember to include the appropriate article, especially at the beginning of a sentence.

    NOT:  Last time I saw her, she was going through a divorce.
    BUT:  *The* last time I saw her, she was going through a divorce.
    NOT:  Hour from now when class is over, I'll be a happy man.
    BUT:  *An* hour from now when class is over, I'll be a happy man.

# Problems with Connecting Words •

Prepositions, conjunctions, and other miscellaneous words and phrases work to clarify relationships among the various parts of our sentences. Most of the time they do their job quietly, causing us few problems. But if we misuse them or forget to include them, we—or our readers—will discover how vital they are to successful communication. So here are some pointers.

## • Prepositions

1. In many idiomatic expressions, especially in spoken English, the preposition may be implied or understood.

> Classes start Monday.
>
> (*on* is implied)

But in formal writing, you are usually better off including all prepositions.

> *In* January, I will finish my degree.
> Prices are expected to rise *during* the next five years.

2. Many verbs, called phrasal verbs, require specific prepositions or adverbs to complete their meaning; some may even change meaning drastically when a different term is substituted.

> After hanging *up* the phone, she hung *around* the house.
> They usually hang *out* at the shopping mall. Hang *in* there!

Be sure to include all appropriate phrasal terms, especially when using compound verbs.

> INCOMPLETE:  I counted but finally despaired *of* getting a vacation.
> COMPLETE:    I counted *on* but finally despaired *of* getting a vacation.
> INCOMPLETE:  They passed an ambulance which was either coming or going *to* an accident.
> COMPLETE:    They passed an ambulance which was either coming *from* or going *to* an accident.

## • Conjunctions

1. Choose the best conjunction for your purposes. The coordinating conjunction *and* is versatile but often overworked. Try using *but* to provide contrast, *so* and *for* to emphasize a cause-effect relationship.

> INEFFECTIVE:  She picked up a magazine *and* soon got bored and put it down.
> EFFECTIVE:    She picked up a magazine *but* soon got bored and put it down.
> INEFFECTIVE:  The plants in the garden were drooping, *and* it hadn't rained in two weeks.

> EFFECTIVE: The plants in the garden were drooping, *for* it hadn't rained in two weeks.
>
> EFFECTIVE: The plants in the garden were drooping, *so* I got out the hose.

Don't forget that subordinating conjunctions such as *although, because, if, when, after,* etc. can suggest both the relationship between your ideas and their relative importance.

> INEFFECTIVE: I took a course in political theory, *and* now I find the front page of the newspaper much more interesting.
>
> EFFECTIVE: *After* taking a course in political theory, I find the front page of the newspaper much more interesting.

2. The word *that* sometimes serves as a subordinating conjunction. (We have seen it before as a demonstrative adjective—*That* man is following me—and as a pronoun—Stop *that*!)

   As a conjunction it is often left out, especially if the sentence is short.

> According to the song, the man [that] she loved was untrue.

Sometimes, though, you need to supply the conjunction to avert potential misreading.

> CONFUSING: She told the police detectives had been following her for a week.
>
> CLEAR: She told the police *that* detectives had been following her for a week.
>
> CONFUSING: I have discovered only a few executives really understand computers and what they can do.
>
> CLEAR: I have discovered *that* only a few executives really understand computers and what they can do.

# • Comparisons

1. Make your comparisons complete. If you are evaluating an item, you need to supply the context against which it is being measured.

> INCOMPLETE: I find *better fruit* at my local grocery store.
>
> COMPLETE: I find *better fruit* at my local grocery store *than I do at the supermarket.*
>
> INCOMPLETE: E.T. was *the best movie*!
>
> COMPLETE: E.T. was *the best movie I saw all year.*

**NOTE:** Product advertisements often deliberately break this rule:

Chompies have better taste, better nutrition—your dog will love them!

(Better than what? They are hoping you won't ask.)

2. Make sure that your comparison matches two or more items that are truly comparable.

ILLOGICAL: She found that a *pilot's job* was more exciting and better paid than a *teacher*, so she switched careers.
LOGICAL: She found that a *pilot's job* was more exciting and better paid than a *teacher's job* [or than *that of a teacher*], so she switched careers.

3. Watch out for ambiguous comparisons. If necessary, rewrite them to spell out what is being compared to what.

AMBIGUOUS: I dislike that professor more than Mr. Weston.

(Do you dislike the professor more than you dislike Mr. Weston? Or do you dislike the professor more than Mr. Weston does?)

CLEAR: I dislike that professor more than I do Mr. Weston.
CLEAR: I dislike that professor more than Mr. Weston does.

4. When comparing two items, make it clear whether they belong to the same general class of items or to different classes.

   a. When two items belong to the same class, include the clue words *other*, *any other*, or *else*.

   She is more competent than *other* people in my shop.
   She is more competent than *any other person* in my shop.
   She is more competent than anyone *else* in my shop.

   b. When the items belong in different classes, use the clue word *any*.

   Jack got a higher salary than *any* of the construction workers.
   (Here Jack is not a construction worker.)

5. When using the word *as* to phrase your comparison, be sure to use it twice.

COMMON SENTENCE FAULTS

NOT:  That hotel in Rome was expensive *as* the Ritz.
BUT:  That hotel in Rome was *as* expensive *as* the Ritz.
NOT:  She laughed *as* hard, if not harder than I did.
BUT:  She laughed *as* hard *as*, if not harder than I did.

or

She laughed *as* hard *as* I did, if not harder.

# FOUR

# Effective Writing: Sentences and Paragraphs

## Combining Ideas More Effectively •

Sentence effectiveness concerns economy, clarity, precision, and fluidity in the expression of thoughts. The more economically, clearly, precisely, and fluidly we express our thoughts, the more easily a reader can follow the flow of ideas and understand the content of the text. Of course, it's easy for an instructor to demand these qualities—they sound quite sensible—but how should we apply these ideas actively in our writing?

Economy does not require that all sentences be without color and detail; precision does not preclude creative use of language; clarity does not disallow subtlety, just as fluidity does not keep us from using short, to-the-point, sometimes abrupt phrasing. What these principles do require is that we pick and choose our words carefully, that we mean exactly what we say we mean, and that we weave our information into pleasing, easily grasped units.

Important to the process of consolidating ideas, of weaving bits and pieces of information together, are **coordination** and **subordination**.

# • Coordination

**Coordination** involves combining words, phrases and clauses by means of coordinating connectors. Coordinating conjunctions (the FANBOYS— *for, and, nor, but, or, yet, so*) and correlative conjunctions (*both-and, either-or, neither-nor, not-but, not only-but also*) can join words, phrases, or clauses whereas conjunctive adverbs (*however, therefore, moreover, consequently, furthermore, otherwise, then*, etc.) can link main clauses only. (For more information on connecting words, see Chapter One, p. 34.)

REMEMBER: Conjunctive adverbs require a semicolon when they introduce a second main clause.

The following are examples of **coordinated** elements:

The policeman who gave me the speeding ticket was *merciless but charming*. (coordinated adjectives)

The dog *barked and growled* at the strange image, not realizing that he was looking into a mirror. (coordinated verbs)

*Neither the residents nor the merchants approved of the new zoning laws. (coordinated subjects)*

When we had fights, my brother always *hit me first and asked questions later*. (coordinated predicates)

*Swaying to and fro, yet somehow avoiding collision*, the drunk stumbled through the crowd. (coordinated participle phrases)

He *not only insulted me, but also stepped on my toes while we were dancing*. (coordinated predicates)

*Not only did he insult me, but he also stepped on my toes while we were dancing*. (same information in coordinated main clauses)

*Everyone attended the meeting; however, nobody signed up for the committee*. (coordinated main clauses)

Good coordination promotes efficiency and precision. When we coordinate such elements as subjects, verbs, adjectives, etc., we save time and space. When we coordinate main clauses, we show clearer relationships between complete thoughts than we would if we had merely placed these thoughts in a long line, one after the other. The following passage, for instance, needs some pruning:

My teacher's voice didn't boom. It didn't screech. It didn't drift soothingly. It didn't sing either. Instead, it beamed its messages down over my shoulder like some alien satellite as I sat, bent over one of the many obligatory play objects in our classroom.

We can get rid of some deadwood and make a more flowing passage by coordinating a few predicates, thereby creating one main image:

My teacher's voice neither boomed, nor screeched, neither drifted soothingly, nor sang, but rather beamed its messages down over my shoulder like some alien satellite as I sat, bent over one of the many obligatory play objects in our classroom.

# •  Subordination

By using **subordination** we can incorporate details and important information into sentences without losing track of the main focus. Subordinating elements may be single modifying words; they may be participle phrases, appositives, absolute phrases; they may be other modifying word groups. (See Chapter One, p. 32.) The information in subordinate constructions may be extremely important to the meaning of the sentence, but it is not the main point of the sentence. In this sense it is subordinate.

The following sentence includes several subordinate elements:

The *neighbor's screaming* children interrupted *Joan's midday* nap.

The writer could use several statements to tell us that Joan had a neighbor with children, that the children were screaming, that Joan was taking a nap at midday, and finally, that the children woke her up. Instead, all of these first bits of information have been reduced to one-word modifiers, leaving the focus on the fact that the children interrupted the nap.

*Breathlessly mumbling some excuse about his dog chewing up the first page*, Harold turned in his research paper.

Again, the writer could use several sentences to give us this information:

Harold mumbled breathlessly to his instructor. He said that his dog chewed up the first page of his research paper, then he turned it in.

However, in the original version, the writer chose to give us the details in an adjective participle phrase, taking out unnecessary wording and leaving the main focus on the moment when Harold turned in the paper.

*When travelling on his expense account*, George always buys the best.

This sentence demonstrates how important, even essential, subordinate material can be. Without the information in the participle phrase, we would assume that George buys the best at all times; with the *when* phrase, we get a quite different impression.

Other examples of subordinated material:

The cat *that ate the canary* died of indigestion.—(adjective clause)
The dealership kept selling cars *even though the salespeople knew that the cars would soon be recalled.*—(adverb clause)
Laura went home sick at noon, *tired of hearing her boss complain about his wife.*—(adjective participle phrase)
The mouse, *a constant visitor in our house*, prefers to take tea in the kitchen.—(appositive phrase)
*After I decide what I'm going to do with my life*, I'm going to take out the trash.—(adverb clause)

## • Using Coordination and Subordination

It is not always easy to move from recognizing subordinate and coordinate constructions to using them effectively in writing. When we write essays and research papers, we are not faced with textbook examples but rather with a series of facts or details which we must group together into sentences. The following series of facts about chimpanzees and human behavior has already been cast into a relatively coherent set of grammatically correct sentences. Still, these sentences are not as effective as they might be in terms of economy and precision.

> Chimpanzees are man's closest living relatives. For this reason, they have been studied by anthropologists for many years. By observing chimpanzees, anthropologists hope to discover things about human behavior. Conflict is an example of shared behavior. It occurs in advanced primate groups in much the same way as in human groups. It is also accompanied, in both cases, by basically similar psychological manifestations.

How can we sort this information into more effective constructions? Clues pointing toward possibilities for subordinating and coordinating information can be seen in word repetitions and linking-verb constructions, as well as in expressions of cause-and-effect, location, time, or other relationships within and between sentences.

For example, in the first three sentences, we see a repetition of the ideas *chimpanzee, anthropologist*, and *chimpanzee/human behavior*. We also see a cause-and-effect relationship expressed in the phrase *for this reason*. These clues can lead us to a method of consolidating this information. (Because the next sentence in the passage begins to deal with the specific idea of *conflict*, it creates a natural break in thoughts; we can disregard the rest of the passage for the moment.)

Let's start by consolidating the information about chimpanzees. Notice that the first statement contains a subject/linking verb/subject complement pattern. (See Chapter One, p. 17.) We can almost always reduce this type of sentence to an appositive phrase, simply by removing the linking verb:

EFFECTIVE WRITING: SENTENCES AND PARAGRAPHS

> Chimpanzees, man's closest living relatives . . .

We now have a noun, followed by a modifying phrase. If we drop the *they* in the next sentence—*they* refers to chimpanzees and so fits in perfectly—we can join the predicate from the second sentence to the subject from the first:

> Chimpanzees, man's closest living relatives, have been studied by anthropologists . . .

Since the next sentence discusses the characteristics of *anthropologists* and since the last word in our new construction is *anthropologist*, we can easily transform the last piece of information in our passage into an adjective clause, thereby completing this phase of the consolidation process:

> Chimpanzees, man's closest living relatives, have been studied by anthropologists, who hope to learn more about human behavior through their observations.

Now we can turn to the next three sentences in the original passage:

> Conflict is an example of shared behavior. It occurs in advanced primate groups in much the same way as in human groups. It is also accompanied, in both cases, by basically similar psychological manifestations.

Immediately, we can see that the subject of all three sentences is *conflict*; again, repetition gives us a clue to the coordination possibilities. One method of joining these sentences is to leave the first sentence as it is and make the subsequent sentences into adjective clauses (*which* clauses in this case). Since the additional statements about conflict are closely related, we can use the correlative conjunctions *not only-but also*:

> Conflict is an example of shared behavior which not only occurs in advanced primate groups in much the same way as in human groups, but is also accompanied, in both cases, by basically similar psychological manifestations.

These revisions represent only one way to improve the effectiveness of the original text; there is no single right way to make a specific passage more effective so long as the sentences connect the ideas logically and blend the harmonious elements.

The following passage also cries out for a bit of coordination/subordination:

> Many students underestimate the value of encyclopedias as reference tools. These students often think that encyclopedias are books suitable

CHAPTER FOUR

only for the preparation of elementary school reports or for leisure
reading. This attitude shows a lack of experience with encyclopedias.
First of all, there are different types of encyclopedias. There are general
encyclopedias and subject encyclopedias. General encyclopedias cover
a broad base of information on a general level. They provide a basic
overview of many subjects. Subject encyclopedias contain more
extensive information pertaining to a more narrow subject area. Some
examples of such subject areas are philosophy, mathematics, technology, computers, literature, etc. The information in these encyclopedias
may be so advanced that a beginner might need to consult a general
work in that subject before being able to understand the text.

By dividing this passage into three main sections according to main
idea—students' feelings about encyclopedias, the description of the general
encyclopedias, and the discussion of the subject encyclopedias—we can
reduce the wordiness quite a bit and improve effectiveness. Let's look at a
revision of the first section:

Many students underestimate the value of encyclopedias as reference
tools, believing that encyclopedias are suitable only for the preparation of
elementary school reports or leisure reading. However, this attitude
shows a lack of experience with encyclopedias.

Notice that, in addition to having consolidated the first two sentences, we
have placed a transition word—*however*—between thoughts. This adds
continuity. The following is a possible revision of the next part of the
passage:

First of all, there are different types of encyclopedias—general and
subject. As the name indicates, general encyclopedias contain a broad
base of general information, providing basic overviews of many subjects.

Here, we've reduced the second sentence to a short appositive and have
combined the third and fourth sentences, subordinating the information in
the fourth into a participle phrase.

The last section can be reduced to one sentence:

Subject encyclopedias—covering more narrow subject areas such as
philosophy, mathematics, technology, computers, and literature—
provide extensive information, which may be so advanced that a beginner
might need to consult a general work on the subject in order to
understand the encyclopedia text.

Again, we've been able to reduce wordiness considerably by combining
information, thus making the passage more effective.

# Problems in Combining Ideas •

Long compound, complex, or compound-complex sentences (see Chapter One, p. 37) must be built organically. Organic sentences grow naturally, out of information which logically belongs together. Artificially constructed sentences, sentences put together solely for the sake of length, will only confuse or frustrate a reader.

The errors most common to complicated sentence constructions are **excessive** coordination or subordination and **inaccurate** coordination or subordination, the second type of error usually involving **faulty parallelism**.

## • Excessive Coordination or Subordination

**Excessive coordination or subordination** occurs in two basic ways. In one, the writer begins a sentence with a main clause, following it up with a long series of loosely related main or subordinate clauses:

> A computerized, electronic typewriter has many electronic functions, but typing on one is not as difficult as many people think because the functions are the same as they are on normal electric or manual typewriters, so it's really just a matter of learning a few commands.

This passage can be improved by resubordinating some clauses and dividing the passage into two main thoughts, one concerning the ease of using the computerized typewriter and the other elaborating on this statement by mentioning how little one must learn to use this typewriter. The rest of the details can be subordinated. The resulting revision:

> Typing on a computerized electronic typewriter is not as difficult as many people think because, even though it may have many electronic functions, most of these are similar to the ones on a normal electric or manual machine; in fact, many times it's just a matter of learning a few basic commands.

This next sentence also contains excessive and loose coordination/subordination:

> Many themes from classic literature have appeared again and again in the literature of later periods, and, in many of these later versions, we can see changes in philosophical standpoint, religious belief, or cultural development because the authors, unconsciously or consciously, have reflected the thinking of their own time while interpreting such characters as Oedipus, Antigone, Orestes, or Phaedra, and by comparing and

CHAPTER FOUR

contrasting the treatments of the same story throughout history, the changes become clear.

A possible revision:

> Many themes from classic literature have appeared again and again in the literature of later periods. Because the authors of these later versions, unconsciously or consciously, have reflected the thinking of their own time while interpreting such characters as Oedipus, Antigone, Orestes, or Phaedra, we can often discover changes in philosophical standpoint, religious belief, or cultural development by comparing and contrasting different treatments of the same story throughout history.

In the revision, we have separated the initial introduction of the subject from the remark we wanted to make about this idea. Instead of stringing several ideas together with *and*, as in the original version, we've decided on one main idea and subordinated the rest of the information. The result is a more cohesive text.

# • Parallelism and Faulty Parallelism

**Parallelism** is a necessary characteristic of good coordination. Usually we create parallel constructions without realizing it. We combine a list of verbs, of adjectives, of prepositional phrases, or of participle phrases because we intuitively tend toward combinations which are harmonious. (For examples of parallel coordinated elements, see *examples of coordinated elements*, Chapter Four, p. 104.) Coordinated elements must not only plug smoothly into the stem part of the sentence, but must also be parallel in form or wording. When a writer coordinates without paying close attention to the exact grammatical forms or the wording of the coordinated elements, **faulty parallelism** can occur.

A good way to test for parallelism is to determine the stem of the sentence; that is, the place where the sentence branches off, and then to compare the coordinated elements closely:

A supervisor's job involves ‖ the assignment of tasks,
‖ the delegation of authority,
‖ and
‖ the arbitration of disputes.

By laying out the sentence in this way, we can easily determine whether or not the coordinated elements (to the right of the vertical lines) are parallel. In this example, each element consists of a noun, followed by a prepositional phrase.

The sentence can also be written in another way:

EFFECTIVE WRITING: SENTENCES AND PARAGRAPHS

Part of a supervisor's job is ‖ to assign tasks,
                                         ‖ to delegate authority,
                                         ‖ and
                                         ‖ to arbitrate dispute.

In the second version, the coordinated elements are infinitive phrases. Both types of elements function well in their respective sentences; the important thing to remember in writing parallel constructions is that once a type of phrasing has been chosen, it must be used consistently. The sentence stems may also appear at the end of the sentence, as in the following example:

Assigning tasks, ‖
delegating authority, ‖
and
arbitrating disputes ‖ are all parts of a supervisor's job.

Now, let's consider some cases of **faulty parallelism** and some possible revisions:

The small boy *shouted, screamed*, and *then there was a whimpering* after his mother took the dead fish from under his pillow.

The three coordinated elements in this sentence are two verbs followed by a main clause; they are therefore unparallel.
   One revision might be:

The small boy *shouted, screamed*, and then *whimpered* after his mother took the dead fish from under his pillow.

Another example:

Stan gets his work done by *sitting* at his desk with his feet up, *going* out for lunch, and *gives* the assignment to one of his subordinates.

The coordinated elements here, two gerund phrases (objects of the preposition *by*) and one complete predicate, are again unparallel.
   A possible revision:

Stan gets his work done by *sitting* at his desk with his feet up, *going* out for a long lunch, and finally *giving* the assignment to one of his subordinates.

Parallel constructions containing correlative conjunctions create special problems. In the case of correlative pairs (*both-and, either-or, neither-nor, not-but, not only-but also*) the elements following the two coordinators must be parallel to each other.

For example:

> The person who robbed that bank and didn't get caught is *either* very clever *or* very lucky.

By using the same kind of diagram we saw earlier in the chapter, we can discover and compare the correlative elements:

> The person who robbed that bank and didn't get caught is . . .
> either ‖ very clever
> or      ‖ very lucky.

We can see that each element contains a correlative conjunction and an adverb/adjective modifying phrase.

The following sentence, on the other hand, contains a parallelism error:

> My boss will *either* promote me for the work I did on this job *or* he'll fire me.

A diagram will point out the error:

> My boss will either ‖ promote me for the work I did on this job.
>          or        ‖ he'll fire me.

The first correlative conjunction is followed by a predicate and the second conjunction in the pair is followed by an entire main clause; therefore, the sentence is unparallel.

Possible revisions:

> *Either* my boss will promote me for the work I did on this job *or* he'll fire me.
> My boss will *either* promote me *or* fire me for the work I did on this job.

In the first revision the coordinated elements are main clauses; in the second they are predicates.

# Emphasis •

An important aspect of sentence effectiveness is **emphasis**. The most basic kind of emphasis requires the writer to decide which kind of information should be included in the main clause(s) of a sentence and which information should be placed in subordinate constructions. These choices influence

EFFECTIVE WRITING: SENTENCES AND PARAGRAPHS

accuracy as well as emphasis. The following sentence represents a case of inaccurate subordination:

When I called the veterinarian, I noticed my parakeet's beak-rash.

In all likelihood, the pet owner saw the beak-rash first and *then* called the veterinarian. If the sentence is to reflect this sequence accurately, it should read

When I noticed my parakeet's beak-rash, I called the veterinarian.

Ineffective subordination may distort *emphasis* in more subtle ways:

The car hit the boy before it sped away.

This sentence may be technically accurate, but we need to look at the emphasis. It is obviously important that the car hit the boy, a fact which supports its placement in a main clause; however, this combination of events, placed in one sentence, points not just to an accident but to a case of hit-and-run. This criminal aspect of the event is probably the most dramatic, the one we want our readers to react to morally and emotionally. The car's speeding away is, therefore, at least as important as the boy's being hit and should show at least grammatic equality:

The car hit the boy, and then it sped away.

It could even become the main point of the sentence:

After the car hit the boy, it sped away.

This last version would be especially appropriate in a newspaper article reporting the accident and emphasizing the crime.
REMEMBER: If you have an emphatic point to make, don't subordinate it.

## Cumulative and Periodic Sentences

Once we've decided which elements belong in which kind of clause or phrase, we still have the option of ordering movable elements to achieve desired emphasis. In a complex sentence, for example, we often have a choice of putting the main clause before the subordinate clause or of placing the subordinate clause before the main clause. A sentence which first states the main thought and then adds or accumulates details is called a **cumulative sentence**. A sentence which states the main idea at the end is a **periodic sentence**.

The next example follows the more common pattern of the two, that of the cumulative sentence:

CHAPTER FOUR

> Jill suddenly remembered that she'd left her passport in one of her
> suitcases after she'd deposited her luggage at the flight check-in counter.

Does the main clause work effectively as it stands, before the subordinate clause? Perhaps the sentence would become more humorous if we are told about the passport after we learn that Jill has already given up her luggage:

> After she'd deposited her luggage at the flight check-in counter, Jill
> suddenly remembered that she'd left her passport in one of the suitcases.

In this second version, a periodic sentence, the reader follows the natural chain of events (depositing . . . remembering) and can perhaps better recreate Jill's moment of horror.

With emphasis, as with coordination and subordination, we often have many choices available. We may come up with diverse solutions, but we should make our choices consciously, considering both the intended meaning and the desired effect.

## Movable and Non-movable Phrases

The same decision-making process applies to movable phrases. It is important, in all cases, to distinguish between **movable** and **non-movable** phrases and clauses: a non-movable phrase or clause is one whose change of position results in a misplaced modifier:

> The pear *lying in the middle of the table* had a worm.
> The pear had a worm *lying in the middle of the table.*

In this example, the adjective participle phrase *lying in the middle of the table* is non-movable. The first sentence pictures a worm in a pear, which is, in turn, lying on a table; the second sentence pictures a worm which, although it actually belongs to or in the pear, is lying on the table, possibly all by itself. Now let's consider the following sentence:

> The zebra finch screeched his abrasive love song, *looking longingly out
> into the garden.*

Because the adjective participle phrase can refer only to the zebra finch and cannot logically confuse the sentence by changing positions, it constitutes a movable phrase. Therefore, we can decide where to place the phrase on the basis of emphasis.

The most emphatic part of a sentence is the end. Like the punch-line of a joke, the moral of a fable, or the final score of a baseball game, what comes last often lingers in our minds the longest. The second most emphatic part of a sentence is the opening—that which we see first. The least emphatic

EFFECTIVE WRITING: SENTENCES AND PARAGRAPHS

part of a sentence is the middle. With this information in mind, we can look at the various possibilities for the zebra finch sentence:

> The zebra finch screeched his abrasive love song, *looking longingly out into the garden.*
> or:
> *Looking longingly out into the garden,* the zebra finch screeched his abrasive love song.
> or:
> The zebra finch, *looking longingly out into the garden,* screeched his abrasive love song.

Each version places a slightly different emphasis on the action of looking out into the garden.

## General Qualifiers

Other phrases which can be moved are general qualifiers such as *in my opinion, for the most part,* and *as a rule.* Although they can usually appear at the beginning, in the middle, or at the end of a sentence, they tend to work better in the middle or at the beginning. Consider the following sentence:

> The new zoning law will result in the total disintegration of the residential character of the neighborhood, *in my opinion.*

Placed at the end of the sentence, in the most emphatic position, the phrase *in my opinion* undercuts the power of the statement and adds an almost apologetic note. Placed at the beginning, it still retains emphasis, but leaves the statement in the spotlight:

> *In my opinion,* the new zoning law will result in the total disintegration of the residential character of the neighborhood.

Placed in the middle, it represents an obligatory qualifying statement which the speaker would like to play down:

> The new zoning law, *in my opinion,* will result in the total disintegration of the residential character of the neighborhood.

## However

One word which needs particularly careful placing is *however.* We often find it at the beginning of a clause or sentence where it provides an adequate transition between ideas; more often than not, however, it will be more emphatic later in the clause. *However* signals a contrast; place the word after the item of contrast if you can.

The newspaper blew away; the book, *however*, stayed on the bench.

Here we have emphasized the different fates of the newspaper and the book.

He was a cute little boy at age five; when he grew up, *however*, he became repulsive.

Here we have emphasized the two different periods of the boy's life.

## Lists

Items in a **list** make up another class of movable elements. When we write lists for ourselves (for example, "Things to do"), we have many possibilities for highlighting the most important items on the list: we can underline them; we can use indentations; we can use asterisks; or we can write in different colors. In most formal texts, however, we can employ very few visual aids in emphasizing words. Italics, for example, must be used sparingly and in very specific instances. Therefore, we must rely on word order to show our readers what is important.

As in a sentence, the most emphatic part of a list is the last element. It is the culmination of our list and will, merely because of its placement, probably be remembered a little longer. Therefore, in a list where there is no other ordering factor (such as chronology), the most important elements should come last. Also if the list has a progression, the elements should show that progression. Any type of organization helps readers retain content:

When I arrived at my final, I realized that I'd forgotten my pencil, I'd spilled coffee on my notebook, and I'd come on the wrong day.

The comic character of this sentence depends on the build-up of blunders from minor to major.

We expect lists to follow a logical order as well. Think of how odd it would have sounded to Caesar's public had he said:

I conquered, I saw, I came.

When making lists, remember to identify and reinforce progression through placement and, in general, place the most important elements last.

# Variety •

Once we've decided how information should be combined and where points of emphasis should fall, we can start to think about varying our sentences. Any student, whether in a university, a technical institute, or a business school, can testify to the effects of the deadly monotone. Speakers who never vary the rhythm of their statements, who never change tone of voice, or who don't use gestures, will certainly put their listeners to sleep within a very short time. As writers, we are even more limited in our possibilities to entertain and interest the receivers of our thoughts because we can use neither voice nor gesture. Therefore, we need to remember the importance, not only of well-organized, clear, precise writing, but of writing with variety—especially in the length and structure of our sentences. For example, a text made up of only long, complicated, dense sentences will soon tax a reader's concentration:

> This graduating class, the ninety-eighth that our high school has seen, faces, as do all young people today, a great challenge, one that, despite all progress and technological advances, remains the great problem to which each generation must address itself. If we look into the past, we find that, although the answers have come and gone, the problem, true to its immortal nature, reasserts itself again and again, in the most varied of historical concepts . . .

If this address remains at this level, the students may fall asleep before they find out what their great challenge is. On the other hand, a passage containing only short, simple, primer-style sentences will quickly send the reader of normal endurance up the walls or at least out the door:

> We travelled continuously for two days. The train was delayed at the Yugoslavian border. It was also delayed at every small town in Yugoslavia. It was an express train. Still, it stopped at every town. There is a reason for this. All foreign trains must stop to pick up and transport commuters. It's part of the agreement between the foreign railroads and the Yugoslavian government. The foreign trains may use the tracks for a low fee. However, they have to provide commuter service for local traffic. We arrived in Athens eight hours late.

Both of these passages are relatively extreme cases; they show, however, that we really do need more than grammatical correctness in our writing. We need balance and variety. Certain sentences must take on one form or another for reasons of content (to give proper emphasis to main ideas, avoid misplaced modifiers, to express chronology, etc.). Still, in many cases, it's not going to be that important if certain information appears in a prepositional phrase, an adjective or adverb phrase, or in a subordinate clause of some type. In these cases, we can use the principle of variety to structure our sentences.

The following passage is a narrative describing a spelling bee. Keeping sentence variety in mind, let's look at some of the possibilities for combining ideas (coordinating and subordinating).

CHAPTER FOUR

The quarterly spell-downs traditionally took place during one of the Friday school assemblies. They showed a level of rivalry and tension comparable to those produced by the arena events in ancient Rome. We stood on the stage of the school auditorium like puny gladiators. We were spurred on to battle by indifferent commanders who were more interested in the spectacle of their own achievement and power than in any aesthetic or educational experience on our part. We looked at our feet. We glanced feverishly out at the sea of faces in the audience. We tried not to see our friends or our enemies. Finally we furtively peeked at each other and were joined in weak-kneed anticipation and anxiety. Our hearts pounded. Our voices wavered. Nevertheless, we learned to respond to the adrenaline rush of competition. Some of us even learned to spell.

Notice the repetition of the straightforward, short, simple sentences, the lack of introductory material preceding main clauses, and the general lack of participle phrases. We can create *variety* by transforming some of these main clauses into modifying phrases and moving them into other, related sentences.

For example:

The quarterly spell-downs, *traditionally taking place during one of the Friday school assemblies*, showed a level of rivalry and tension comparable to those produced by the arena events in Rome. We stood on the stage of the school auditorium like puny gladiators, *spurred on to battle by indifferent commanders who were more interested in the spectacle of their own achievement and power than in any aesthetic or educational experience on our part*. We looked at our feet or glanced feverishly out at the sea of faces, *trying not to see our friends—or our enemies*. Finally, *joined in weak-kneed anticipation and anxiety*, we furtively peeked at each other. Our hearts pounded; our voices wavered; yet we learned to respond to the adrenalin rush of competition. Some of us even learned to spell.

With relatively few changes, we have made the narrative much more varied and interesting. By combining and subordinating, we've condensed and, therefore, intensified the description; by adding participle phrases, we've varied the rhythm. Notice how the dash also creates a pause and enhances the visual effect of the scene. Again, this narrative could have been revised in many ways—this is merely one possibility.

## VARIETY CREATES INTEREST

# Diction •

Language does not exist in a vacuum but takes place in specific contexts. We constantly shift the tone, style, and structure of our language to respond to various situations. When we speak to our children, we use a different language from the one we use when speaking to our bosses; teenagers speak one language among themselves, another with their teachers. How many parents have been confused by expressions ranging from *far out*, to *uptight*, to *gnarly* and *bad*?

In the same way, we need to make shifts in written language when writing academic papers or professional reports. We need to use a standardized language with more rigid rules than are necessary in everyday speech and casual writing. After all, when we speak to each other, we have the opportunity of watching our listeners; if we see puzzled or threatening looks on their faces, we can always back up and re-explain or clarify what we've just said. When we submit an academic or professional piece of writing, however, we send it out to unknown readers, readers with differing or perhaps even diametrically opposed opinions. In these cases there is no room for jargon or for vague, casual and slang-filled writing. Our message must be clear and precise. They have to understand us the first time. We stand or fall according to the strength of what we have already written. Occasions like these call for the use of *formal English*, which must be distinguished from *informal English*.

Like most other questions concerning grammatical aspects of language, the question of what is formal and informal cannot be satisfactorily answered with a rule or single definitive statement. Formal and informal are relative ideas and can be viewed from different perspectives. Still, keys to understanding these concepts exist. Think of the words as they pertain to dress. How many people sit down and ponder what they will wear to a social event which requires informal dress? Can they appear in bathing suits, jogging suits, blazers and slacks or a summer dress? Unless the event were to take place at a swimming pool or a community recreation center, most guests would reject the first two choices. Yet there is enough ambiguity in standards of dress to keep the potential party-goer running from closet to mirror for several hours. If we're willing to spend this much time figuring out what to wear to our next social function, we should be willing to spend a little time figuring out what language we need to use in a formal or informal situation. Neither type of language is more virtuous than the other—each merely serves a different purpose.

## • Formal and Informal English

Another key to the term formal is its root—form. **Formal language** is conscious of form; it is usually more conscious of accuracy and clarity than

CHAPTER FOUR

informal language might be. It strives for precision and balance; nevertheless, it need not be colorless or impersonal.

The following is a passage by writer Bruce Catton[1]; it describes the Civil War General Ulysses S. Grant:

> Grant, the son of a tanner on the Western frontier, was everything Lee was not. He had come up the hard way and embodies nothing in particular except the eternal toughness and sinewy fiber of the men who grew up beyond the mountains. He was one of a body of men who owed reverence and obeisance to no one, who were self-reliant to a fault, who cared hardly anything for the past but who had a sharp eye for the future.
>
> Bruce Catton,
> From *The American Story*

This passage, in formal English, is neither impersonal nor stilted nor boring.

**Informal English** is more intimate; it tends to be more personal and often relies on common experience between speakers for clear communication. When we're talking with good friends or family, people with whom we've shared a great deal of experience, we can usually afford to be fairly relaxed and a bit imprecise—for they know us and are more likely to know what we want to say, even if we don't quite say it precisely. Informal English is the language of letters and discussion; it is often used in poetry and literature to present a realistic and intimate picture of characters in their everyday lives. It is not usually the language of research and academics.

## • Slang and Jargon

Other elements to be aware of and to use or avoid consciously and deliberately are **slang** and **jargon**. Slang—creative, colorful, improvisational, and often rebellious or anarchistic—consists of language with meaning for a specific group. It identifies us with a certain group of people, with a specific region, age group, social class, or even ideology. We achieve community through the use of slang; we can even use it to keep outsiders from understanding exactly what we're saying. For all of these reasons, slang has very limited possibilities for effective use in formal writing. When we write for a broad audience, and most formal expository writing seeks a broad audience, we want to avoid using words which readers won't understand or which might make them feel closed-out or excluded.

The same holds true for jargon. Useful within a specialized field, terminology must be invented all the time for new areas of science and technology. However, such language becomes a barrier when used in writing meant to communicate to people outside of the specialized field.

---

[1]"Grant and Lee: A study in contrasts" by Bruce Catton, from *The American Story* ed. by Earl Schenck Miers 1956. Copyright U.S. Capitol Historical Society. All rights reserved. Used with permission.

# •  Pretentious Diction

Even more ineffective than slang and jargon is **pretentious diction**. Anyone who has ever listened to a lecture or read a book which uses overly complex language or unnecessarily complicated vocabulary can attest to the aggravation of pretentious language. If we can use simple, direct words, we should probably do so and give our readers a fighting chance to grasp our meaning.

For example, a conversation between Student Slang and Professor Pretentious might not be communication after all:

S: Hey dude. So what's goin' on with homework? I was so psyched on Monday . . . I couldn't make History.
P: I'm uncertain as to what you intend with your salutation. I find, however, a modicum of disrespect in such greetings.
S: Yaaw. That's one gnarly mouthpiece your got there, doc.
P: Perhaps you'd care to explicate?
S: Sure, I'd explicate if I had time, but I gotta jam.
P: Your gesticulations indicate the import of this last statement; I take it we shall remark one another in a more academic environment, shall we say Wednesday at ten?
S: Whatever, doc. But I'll see ya in class.
P: Farewell, Slang.
S: Later, dude . . . much.

Neither of these two characters seems too interested in communicating with the other. Formal English is sometimes helpful in that it creates a neutral ground where everyone has some chance of understanding what's going on.

A related stylistic problem concerns **euphemisms**, those "polite" words or phrases which writers sometimes substitute for direct expressions which they fear might offend their audience. In some situations, of course, such sensitivity is justified, but if overused, euphemisms will make your prose sound affected and coy. Consider the following variations:

She is down in the dumps because recently her father croaked.
She is very depressed because recently her father died.
She is unutterably melancholy because recently her father passed on to his reward.

The use of slang in the first sentence is clearly inappropriate in the context. *Depressed* and *died* are simple statements of fact. But *unutterably melancholy* is pretentious and *passed on to his reward* is an unnecessary euphemism.

## •  Cliché

A **cliché**, an expression which has become tired and worn through overuse, causes another kind of problem—boredom. Any woman who has read old romantic novels or romances, or has watched older Hollywood movies, might be bored and a little insulted if her lover compared her teeth to *pearls*, lips to *rubies* or eyes to *two limpid pools*. A man, on the other hand, may no longer like to be thought of as the *strong, silent type* who is *solid as a rock*. These phrases might have been interesting the first time they were used, but they've seen better days—no one wants to be thought of as just another cliché. Along the same lines, readers like to feel that a writer has taken some time, imagination, and effort in writing a text or creating an image. Making our language accessible, understandable and yet fresh and innovative is one of the most challenging of our tasks as writers.

**NOTE:** When sitting down to write, ask yourself whether the situation demands informal or formal language; then choose your words accordingly. In general, try to avoid slang words, jargon, pretentious language and cliché expressions. Strive instead for those words which will communicate your thoughts as clearly, precisely, directly, and vividly as possible. If in doubt about the appropriateness of an individual word or phrase, consult a good, up-to-date dictionary (one which includes usage labels) or check the *Glossary of Usage* in Appendix A.

# Paragraphs •

Many developing writers use paragraphs haphazardly, responding only to some vague feeling that it's time to indent. For readers, getting through a text written on this principle may be like driving-through Manhattan without a map. They may arrive at the appropriate destination, but be confused during the trip. Logically ordered paragraph divisions, on the other hand, let readers know where they are in the text; given these signposts, they can trace the route of the writer's thought with greater ease.

The paragraph is not an arbitrary unit, but one that responds to guidelines of form and content. These guidelines will vary, depending on the type of writing concerned. Much journalistic writing, for example, must provide a great deal of information in a limited space. For this reason, the sentences tend to be condensed and to the point; the flow of information is rapid. Newspaper paragraphs, reflecting this need for compression, are also short and tightly-packed. Fiction, on the other hand, follows other guidelines. The novelist or story writer may follow self-imposed rules of style or may paragraph intuitively and experimentally. Leisurely descriptive para-

EFFECTIVE WRITING: SENTENCES AND PARAGRAPHS

graphs may last a whole page, then give way to one or two-line paragraphs of dialogue.

Expository writing, the type of writing most often found in academic reports, research papers, and critical essays, follows its own guidelines. Like newspaper writing, it is geared to a broad audience and, therefore, demands a consistency of language and predictability of style not required of fiction. Because it attempts not only to inform, but often to analyze or explain difficult and complex concepts, expository prose must communicate in a clear, methodical fashion.

Clear communication requires regularized grammar and punctuation, well-constructed, effective sentences, and a standardized use of language—formal English. The next requirement of clear communication concerns the **paragraph**. Good paragraphs result from the logical grouping and ordering of ideas, the smooth flow from one idea to the next, and the adequate elaboration of general statements. These principles of paragraph writing are called **unity**, **coherence**, and **development**.

# •   Unity

**Unity** is the most basic principle of good paragraph writing. A unified paragraph follows one central or **controlling idea**. This controlling idea can be implied though it is usually stated directly in a **topic sentence**. Each sentence in the paragraph must support or follow from this controlling idea.

Let's consider the following group of sentences with the idea of forming a unified paragraph:

1.  The *xonta* was the traditional family dwelling of the Hupa Indians before the twentieth century.
2.  It took up a surface area of approximately twenty square feet.
3.  It was made of cedar planking.
4.  It was built partly underground and partly above-ground.
5.  The women and small children usually slept there.
6.  It was used to store the family's belongings.
7.  The men slept in another kind of structure called the *taikyuw*.
8.  The *taikyuw* was a sweathouse, designed to retain heat.
9.  The men also worked in the *taikyuw*.
10. The entryways of the *xonta* all faced the same mountain.
11. These entryways were kept small so that bears couldn't get in.
12. There were a lot more bears in Northern California then than there are now.

Assuming that the first sentence contains our controlling idea, we must consider which of the remaining sentences we would include in a paragraph describing the *xonta*.

All except sentences seven, eight, nine, and twelve deal directly with characteristics of the xonta and could, therefore, belong in our paragraph. Sentences seven, eight, and nine really belong in another paragraph describing the *taikyuw*. If we wanted to include information on both dwellings in one paragraph, we could do so, but first, we would have to modify the controlling idea. Such a modification could be:

> The Hupa Indians traditionally used two forms of dwelling—the *xonta* and the *taikyuw*.

If this were our topic sentence, we could use all sentences in this example except for number twelve, which drifts away from the subject completely.

**NOTE:** To achieve unity in your own paragraphs, use the following three-point checklist:

1. Identify your controlling idea.

2. Put that idea into a clear, well-focused topic sentence—preferably at or near the beginning of the paragraph.

3. Check the other sentences in the paragraph against this topic sentence. Each sentence should develop the controlling idea. Delete any sentence that does not.

## •  Coherence

**Coherence** is the principal that relates ideas to one another, both within a paragraph and from one paragraph to the next. There are two main aspects of coherence: organizing or **ordering** ideas and **connecting** these ideas into a smooth, flowing train of thought.

We can see the principles behind the first aspect, the ordering of ideas, by examining some everyday situations.

Someone wanting to describe a chain of events will probably start at a particular point in time and move forward. The description of a journey, the analysis of an historical event, the discussion of a social trend or another development could all be organized chronologically, for example. The order may occasionally be interrupted or reversed for reasons of suspense or thematic development (like flashbacks in movies) and still follow the organizing principle of chronology. Thus **time order** is one of the principles which we may use to organize information into paragraphs.

**Space** can also be a criterion for organizing a paragraph, especially a paragraph of static description. Here it might be helpful to think of the way a movie camera shows us a landscape. Although the camera may move slowly from left to right, from right to left, from up to down, etc., depending on the purpose of the scene, it will inevitably begin at one point and move, in a methodical fashion, in one direction or the other. We can use the same principle when describing places or objects, beginning at one point

EFFECTIVE WRITING: SENTENCES AND PARAGRAPHS

and moving methodically to the next. Like the camera we can describe a room or a person tracking right to left, left to right, from top to bottom, from inside to out, etc.

One of the most common ways to order thoughts is to move from the **general to the particular** or the **particular to the general**. If someone asks us how we liked a play, we will probably start out with a general statement ("Fantastic," "Boring," "Mediocre") and then give the details (information about the plot, the acting, the lighting, the stage design, and so on). We most often move from the general to the particular in writing critical essays, research papers, and reports. We make statements, and then we back them up with particulars. However, we can also move from the particular to the general if we like. Thinking of the same instance concerning the play, we could decide to describe various particular criticisms ("The acting was awful. Everyone kept forgetting lines and missing entrances") and then slowly move toward a general statement about the play ("All-in-all it was pretty mediocre"). Although we tend to use the general to the particular more, either works well as a principle for organizing thoughts into easily comprehended sequences.

We have many options for organizing our thoughts; what is important is that we develop a plan and follow it. If we had to develop our sentences about the *xonta* and the *taikyuw* (p. 123) into a paragraph, for example, we might start with the suggested topic sentence—a general statement—and then move into the details of construction and use first the *xonta* type of dwelling and then the other.

> The Hupa Indians traditionally used two forms of dwelling—the xonta and the taikyuw. The xonta was the traditional family dwelling. It served as a shelter for the women and children. It was also a storage place for the family belongings. It was made of cedar planking; it covered a surface area of approximately twenty square feet and was built partly underground and partly above-ground. The entrances were small and faced a mountain near the village. The taikyuw was a sweathouse, designed to retain heat. It had little ventilation. The men worked here. They also slept in the taikyuw.

Having decided on a general order, we are now ready to consider the second principle of good coherence: the flow of ideas and the smooth transition from one thought to the next.

Much of this fluidity can be achieved by coordinating and subordinating effectively, as well as by varying sentence patterns. The last touch can often be provided by a few **transitional words** or phrases to guide the reader from one thought to the next. If we revised the paragraph above with these principles in mind, we might arrive at something like the following:

> The Hupa Indians traditionally used two forms of dwelling—the xonta and the taikyuw. The xonta, the traditional family dwelling, served not only as

a shelter for the women and children, but also as a storage place for the family belongings. Made of cedar planking, it was built partly above-ground and partly underground and covered a surface area of approximately twenty square feet. Each xonta had a small entrance which faced one particular mountain near the village. The taikyuw, on the other hand, was the place where the men worked and slept. Like the xonta, it was a structure built partly above-ground, partly underground; unlike the xonta, however, it was designed as a sweathouse and, therefore, had little ventilation.

In this revision, we have combined single fact clauses into compound constructions wherever possible. In addition, we've provided such transitional markers as *on the other hand, like the xonta,* and *however.* All of these changes help the paragraph read more smoothly.

# • Development

We're now ready to deal with the last of our paragraph skills—**development**. After we've made sure that our paragraphs are unified and coherent, we have to check to make sure that we've developed our ideas sufficiently to get our point across.

Going back to everyday situations, we can easily see the importance of development. If we hear a friend say, "I hate my new job," the first thing we're going to ask is, "Why?" If the friend answers, "Lots of reasons," we're probably going to ask, "What reasons?" We are very seldom satisfied with such general statements when thinking about important situations or topics. We want to know the details. If friends tell us that the film they just saw was horrible or that a particular vacation spot is overrated, we want to know why. People reading our written ideas are not going to be any different: they'll want to know the reasons behind our judgments, the evidence supporting our generalizations.

The same holds true for pictures that we're trying to communicate. If we write about a "beautiful landscape," what will our readers imagine—a coastline, a mountain lake, a glacier, a suburban residential area? Our pictures may be clear to us, but without the details, we're not going to transmit them to our readers.

Let's look at our sample paragraph again with the idea of development in mind. We've made sure that all of the sentences belong in the paragraph; we've organized them logically and smoothed out the flow of ideas—but do we have enough details? Are any important facts unclear or missing altogether? One thing we might notice is that there is more physical information about the xonta than the taikyuw. Questions that might occur to a reader are: Is the taikyuw the same size as the xonta or bigger? What do we mean by little ventilation? Did the xonta have means of ventilation other than the entrance? Was the taikyuw made of the same materials?

The following is a final draft of this paragraph in which we can see an improvement in *development*:

> The Hupa Indians traditionally used two forms of dwelling—the xonta and the taikyuw. The xonta, the traditional family dwelling, served not only as a shelter for the women and children, but as a common place for *eating meals* and storing family belongings. Made of cedar planking, it was built part above-ground and part underground and covered a surface area of approximately twenty square feet. *It had movable planks which could be removed for purposes of ventilation* and a small entrance which usually faced a particular hill near the village. The taikyuw, on the other hand, was the place where the men worked and slept. Like the xonta, it was a structure of *cedar planks* built partly above-ground and partly under-ground; unlike the xonta, however, the taikyuw was designed as a sweathouse, *for which reason the walls were sealed with clay. It was so well insulated that it would stay warm all night without a fire. It had two entrances, one of which faced the river where the men would go after their sweat baths.*

The additional material, indicated by italics, has helped round out this paragraph and make our comparison/contrast of the two dwellings a little more complete.

**NOTE:** To be sure that you have developed your ideas adequately, look again at the controlling idea in each of your paragraphs. What is your purpose, as stated in the topic sentence? Then read each paragraph critically—delete any extraneous material and add whatever facts, examples, or details are still needed to fulfill your purpose.

# Glossary
## of
# Usage

As a writer, you alone are responsible for the words you use, and people will judge you by your language. Here to help you, then, is a glossary of words and expressions that writers often misuse. Unfortunately, no one can *teach* these words to you; you must learn them yourself through practice. We suggest that you spend time going over these words so that using them correctly will become a habit. Put a check next to the words you have most trouble with; then refer to the glossary every time you use the words until you thoroughly know the correct form. Read through this list periodically (once a term perhaps) to keep the words fresh in your mind.

The glossary points out a variety of different kinds of errors. Some entries simply distinguish between right and wrong spellings or between similarly spelled words. Others concern punctuation errors, specifically errors in the use of the apostrophe. Many entries discuss basic stylistic errors in usage where we are not so much prescribing what is *right and wrong* as advising what contributes to more effective writing. Entries in this category may be inappropriate because they are *pompous* (they try to impress the reader rather than clearly convey an idea), *wordy* (they can be replaced by fewer words), *colloquial* (they are slang and too informal for college writing), *jargon* (they belong to the technical language of a specialized field and are out of place in general writing), or *vague* (the reader cannot tell precisely what the writer means to say).

### Above and beyond, each and every.

Repeating yourself merely dilutes your language. It is more forceful to say *beyond the call of duty* and *each time* than *above and beyond the call of duty* and *each and every time*.

### Accept, except.

To *accept* is a verb meaning to receive; *except*, a preposition, means excluding. You may find yourself less confused if you identify the *ex-* prefix of *except* with the *ex-* of *excluding*. *The post office accepts all letters except those with bombs in them.*

### Advice, advise.

*Advice* is a noun meaning the helpful information one offers to someone else; *advise* is a verb meaning to give this information. *She advised me to go home, but I ignored her advice.*

### Affect, effect.

*Affect* is a verb meaning to influence something. Think of the noun that comes from it—*affection*: I have *affection* for you because you have influenced or *affected* me. *Effect* is usually seen as a noun and means result. Think of *cause and effect*. *Effect* can also be a verb, in the specialized sense of bringing about or completing a change: *He effected my release from jail.*

### All ready, already.

*All ready* means entirely prepared; *already* means previously. *I was all ready to go, but you had already left without me.*

### All right, alright.

Unlike the forms *already* and *altogether*, there is no form *alright*; there is only *all right*. *I feel all right*, that is, entirely fine.

### All together, altogether.

*All together* means in a group, everyone gathered; *altogether* means taken as a whole or on the whole. *The last time the six of us were all together, we drank two bottles of wine each—twelve bottles altogether.*

### A lot, alot.

There is no such word as *alot*. You can remember that *a lot* is two words by keeping in mind the literal meaning: think of a parking lot or the empty lot down the street. When you say, then, that you have *a lot of money*, you mean that you have so much money it could fill a space as big as a parking lot.

GLOSSARY OF USAGE

### Alternate, alternative.

*Alternate* as an adjective means occurring by turns; remember *alternate current*, where the electricity runs back and forth. As a noun, *alternate* means a substitute, and as a verb, to use by turns or to take turns. *The coach alternated between playing the first-string quarterback and his alternate, who had more stamina. Alternative* as an adjective means providing a choice between two things; as a noun it *is* the choice. (*You have no alternative.*)

### Among, between.

Use *between* when referring to two items, *among* for more than two. *I hung the hammock between the two oak trees. The little girl got lost among the tall trees. Between* is used for more than two items, however, when it expresses a reciprocal relationship or the relationship of one thing with several others. *Is there an extradition agreement between the countries of NATO? Put the ketchup between the meat, the potatoes, and the peas.*

### A must.

The use of *must* as a noun (*This course is a must for my degree*) is colloquial and does not belong in college writing. Use *requirement*.

### And/or.

This is a legal expression which it's probably best to avoid in ordinary writing where it will appear as jargon.

### A number of.

Wordy. Why not simply say *some*?

### As, as if.

See *like, as, as if.*

### At this time.

Wordy. Why not just say *now*?

### Because of.

See *due to.*

### Began, begun.

*Began* is the past tense of *begin*; *begun* is the past participle. *I began the job that you had begun earlier.*

### Being that.

Often used colloquially in some areas, but never in formal or semi-formal writing. *I went to bed early because* [not *being that*] *I had had a long day.*

### Between.

See *among, between.*

**Break, brake.**

You can *break* a china plate by dropping it. When a child runs in front of your car, you *brake* quickly by pressing the *brake* pedal.

**Can, may.**

*Can* expresses the ability to do something; *may* expresses permission to do something. *I can walk seven miles in an hour, but I may not walk across the French border without a visa.*

**Character, nature.**

Used unnecessarily in such expressions as *reserved in character* and *work of an important nature*. Say rather, *he is quite reserved* and *she does important work*.

**Close proximity.**

Wordy and repetitious since *proximity* means closeness. Why not simply say *near*?

**Conscious, conscience.**

*Conscious* means being awake, being in possession of your senses; *conscience* is that Jiminy Cricket voice within you that directs you away from evil and towards goodness. One way to remember the difference is to bear in mind that *-ous* is an adjectival ending and *conscious* is an adjective, while *-ence* is a noun ending and *conscience* is a noun. Another way to remember might be to associate *conscious* with *unconscious* and to think of *conscience* as having something to do with *science*: both involve knowing something.

**Continual, continuous.**

*Continual* means repeatedly, over and over; *continuous* means without stopping. Think of a *continuous* line in algebra, a line that has no gaps. Think of the *a* in *continual* as suggesting *again*.

**Could of, may of, might of, should of, would of.**

If you say *could have, may have, might have, should have*, and *would have* fast enough, you'll get *could of, may of, might of, should of*, and *would of*. But this is strictly a sound effect; don't carry it over into your writing.

**Course, coarse.**

*Course* can mean certainly, as in *of course*, or it may refer to a series of classes (*an English course*), a part of a meal (*the first course*), or a direction (*set your course for home*). *Coarse* means rough or uncouth, as in *coarse manners*.

**Criteria, phenomena.**

These words are plural. Their singular forms are *criterion* and *phenomenon*. (See also *data, media*.)

### Data, media.

These are the plural forms of *datum* and *medium*. Even though colloquial usage may permit expressions like *this data is accurate* or *the media makes me sick*, it is best in formal writing to say *these data are accurate* or *the media make me sick*.

### Definitely, definately.

*Definately* is the wrong spelling. Remember that *definitely* is correct by associating the word with *finite*, where the *i* can be clearly heard. Often, however, the word is unnecessary, and rather than adding emphasis, it takes power away from what you are saying. *It was definitely the best beer I ever had*, we might say, but if we say *It was the best beer I ever had*, we focus all the emphasis on best. A person overusing *definitely* sounds insecure, as though needing this intensifier to give strength to empty words.

### Different from, different than.

One thing may *differ from* another; it is, therefore, *different from* the other. *Different than* may seem an easier expression to use, but it is illogical; avoid it.

### Disinterested, uninterested.

*Disinterested* means impartial, not taking a side; *uninterested* means not interested. Because *disinterested* perhaps sounds more important, some writers think they are increasing the weight of their sentence by using the word in place of *uninterested*. Don't make this mistake. *All judges must be disinterested, but even when a trial may be boring, they must not become uninterested.*

### Drank, drunk.

*Drank* is the past tense of *drink, drunk* the past participle. *I drank a glass of juice; I have drunk a glass a day since I was five.*

### Due to.

*Due* is an adjective and should be used as a subject complement (see pp. 17–8): *His cold was due to the rainy weather*. Do not use *due to* to introduce an adverbial phrase when you should use *because of. Because of* [not *due to*] *the rainy weather, he came down with a cold. Due to* sounds more impressive, perhaps, but don't be fooled into using pompous language when, in fact, it's wrong.

### Due to the fact that.

A wordy way of saying *because*. Avoid it whenever you can.

### Each and every.

See *above and beyond.*

**Effect.**

See *affect*.

**Enthuse.**

*Enthuse* as a verb is probably not formal enough for college writing. You may be *enthusiastic*; you may excite *enthusiasm*, but don't *enthuse* or be *enthused*.

**Etc.**

This is an abbreviation for *et cetera*, a Latin expression meaning *and the rest* or *and so forth*. Therefore, it is redundant to say *and etc.* Many people, mispronouncing the expression *ek-setera*, spell the abbreviation *ect.* Don't make this mistake. In any case, use this expression sparingly. It often suggests that you can't be bothered to finish what you're saying or to be more precise. *We traveled through Israel, Jordan, Lebanon, etc.* can be improved by saying, *We traveled through Israel, Jordan, Lebanon, and other Middle Eastern countries.*

**Except.**

See *accept*.

**Feedback.**

A technical term used by electricians and computer scientists. In most other contexts it is a jargon word.

**Fewer, less.**

Use *fewer* when you are thinking about individual numbers, *less* when thinking about entire amounts. *I have fewer quarters than nickels in my pocket*; *I have less money than I had yesterday. There were fewer objects to my proposal than to yours; my proposal met with less disagreement.*

**Fun.**

*Fun* is not an adjective although it is used as such in informal, colloquial language. It is inappropriate in semi-formal or formal writing to say, for instance, *We had a fun time.* What's wrong with just *having fun*? Better yet, find a more precise and concrete adjective.

**Good, well.**

*Good* is an adjective; *well* is an adverb. The problem of deciding which to use arises in sentences with a linking verb. Should it be *He feels well* or *He feels good*? Solve the problem by considering that we want a word to modify the subject; adjectives modify nouns; therefore we want *good*: *He feels good.* Use *well* when you want to modify a verb: *He listens well*; here we describe not *him* but the way he *listens*. (See pp. 91–2.)

### Hopefully.

*Hopefully* comes from *hopeful*, full of hope. As an adverb, it should modify the verb in the sentence: *he walked hopefully to the mailbox*. But often we misuse *hopefully* to mean *I hope* or *we hope*: *Hopefully you will not have to wait long*, we say, and we mean, *I hope you will not* . . . . Someone the dictionary meaning of the word might change in accordance with popular usage, but until it does, avoid using the word wrongly. Avoid too the awkward construction *it is hoped* . . . . Try something like *with luck* or better yet, be precise: *If the shipment arrives in the next hour, you will not have to wait long*.

### Imply, infer.

*Imply* means to express indirectly. *Infer* means to guess or to come up with a general idea based on an interpretation of the facts. *They implied that it was time for us to leave when they handed us our coats and opened the door. From these indications, we inferred that we had outstayed our welcome.*

### In, into.

*Into* implies an action from outside to inside; *in* implies that something is already there. Think of the difference between a child who jumps *in* the swimming pool and one who jumps *into* the swimming pool.

### In color, in size, in shape, in number.

Unnecessary qualifications when they are obvious. Not *red in color*, but *red*; not *enormous in size*, but *enormous*; not *round in shape*, but *round*; not *few in number*, but *few*.

### Individual.

Don't use this pompous word where the simple word *person* will do.

### Input.

A word from computer language; when used outside its technical meaning, it is likely to be taken as jargon. The word, by the way, is a noun, not a verb.

### Interface.

*Interface*, another noun used in computer language, means a point of meeting; don't overurse it or misuse it where it will be taken as jargon.

### Irregardless.

No such word. You want the simpler (and correct) word *regardless*.

### Its, it's.

*Its* is a possessive pronoun; *it's* is a contraction of *it is*. These words are very often confused, and you may lose the respect of a discerning reader very quickly if you make a mistake here. If in doubt, pause before writing the word and ask yourself, "Do I mean *it is*?" If the answer is yes, then make sure you write *it's*; if the answer is no, then write *its*. (See pp. 22, 56.)

**Lead, led.**

*Lead* (rhyming with *bleed*) is a verb meaning to go before or show the way. The past tense of this verb is *led*. Don't confuse it with the noun *lead* (rhyming with *bed*), which is a metal.

**Less.**

See *fewer, less*.

**Lie, lay.**

*Lie* is an intransitive verb (see pp. 13–4) meaning to rest on something. (*The book lies on the table.*) The past tense of *lie* is *lay*, the past participle, *lain*. *Lay* is a transitive verb meaning to put or place something. (*I lay the book on the table.*) The past tense of *lay* is *laid*, the past participle also *laid*. Thus, *I lay* (not *laid*) *on the bed yesterday*. Catch yourself each time you use one of these forms to check that you're using it correctly. (See also p. 15.)

**Like, as, as if, as though.**

*Like* is a preposition and introduces a prepositional phrase, not a clause. *As, as if*, and *as though* introduce clauses. Thus, *He runs like a cheetah. He runs as* [not *like*] *nobody else can. He ran as if* [or *as though* but not *like*] *he were possessed*.

**Literally.**

*Literally* should be used to stress that the words you're using are indeed true. *I worked from 1:00 until 11:00. It took me literally ten hours to finish the project.* Don't use *literally* when the words are not strictly true. *I literally died laughing*—only a ghost can say this.

**Loose, lose.**

Once you remember that *loose* rhymes with *noose* or *moose*, you will be less likely to confuse this spelling with *lose*, meaning to mislay. Remember that although it is illogical, *lose* rhymes with *choose*.

**Make a choice, make use of, hold a meeting, give advice to.**

Why use three words when one will do? Why not *choose, use, meet, advise*? Not only will you cut down your verbiage, but you will also employ stronger verbs.

**Maximize.**

Like many other pompous, impressive sounding words, *maximize* is often used to hide confusion. To say he *maximized valuable shop resources* sounds mighty impressive, but can you honestly say what this means?

**May.**

See *can, may*.

**Money, monies.**

Don't overuse *monies*. It belongs in the domain of legal or technical language, and although you may think it adds weight to your writing, it will be jargon and thus inappropriate on most ordinary occasions, when *money* will do fine.

**Moral, morale.**

Don't confuse these two words. *Moral*, an adjective referring to good and evil and a noun meaning the lesson at the end of a fable, has the accent on the first syllable. *Morale*, a noun meaning the spirit of a person or a group, has the accent on the second syllable.

**Myself.**

People sometimes use *myself* as a way out of having to choose between *I* or *me*. Learn which pronoun is right for the occasion (see pp. 4–5) and choose it; don't drag in a third pronoun which will be guaranteed wrong. *Both Sgt. White and myself feel that the problem can be corrected* is wrong. Say *Sgt. White and I.* Use *myself* for emphasis (*I grew those tomatoes myself*) or as a reflexive pronoun (*I scratch myself when I itch*).

**Nature.**

See *character, nature*.

**Negative.**

See *positive, negative*.

**Numerous.**

Most of the time this word will sound pompous. Better use *many*.

**Of.**

Often redundant. *The cat went out* [not *out of*] *the window; he stood outside* [not *outside of*] *the bathroom; I found my pen inside* [not *inside of*] *my pocket; she jumped off* [not *off of*] *the diving board.*

**Paid, payed.**

*Paid* is the past tense of *pay*; there is no such spelling as *payed*.

**Perfect.**

See *unique*.

**Personal, personally.**

*My personal favorite* is redundant. *My favorite* is all you need to say. *Personally* often appears in colloquial language when the voice can give it a strong stress, but in more formal writing, it is wordy. *Personally I like older movies best* is less emphatic than *I like older movies best*, where all the emphasis can fall on *I*.

## Personal, personnel.

*Personal* has to do with people, with, of course, *persons*. *Personnel* has only two uses: employees and members of the military. It is probably best to treat *personnel* as a technical military word; thus, although you would speak in a military context of, say, *enlisted personnel*, in ordinary writing you'd be better off speaking of *enlisted people*.

## Phenomena.

See *criteria, phenomena*.

## Plus.

*Plus* should not be used as a noun. Avoid expressions such as *It was a plus for his career*. Say more precisely how it actually helped his career. Used as a conjunction, *plus* is often a weak transitional word; all it tells the reader is that you are putting two thoughts together; it does not tell how these two thoughts fit together. *He worked on the accounts. Plus he made several phone calls*. Find a stronger word to tie these two sentences together. *While he worked . . . ? After he worked . . . ? As a result of working . . . ?* What exactly do you want to say?

## Point in time.

One of the more infamous pompous expressions. Just say *now* or *then*.

## Positive, negative.

Expressions like *a positive experience* and *a negative feeling* are vague. Don't overuse these words; think of a precise word instead.

## Practical, practicable.

*Practical* means helpful; *practicable* means able to be put into practice. *He gave me practical advice; I had to try it out, however, before I knew whether it was practicable*.

## Precede, proceed.

*Precede* means to come before; *proceed* means to continue or carry out an action. *"A" precedes "B" in the alphabet. Even though the police were approaching, the burglars proceeded with the robbery*. Beware of overusing *proceed* in a pompous way. *I proceeded to follow directions* is pompous; just say *I followed the directions*. Not *I proceeded to go to bed* but *I went to bed*.

## Pregnant.

See *unique*.

## Principal, principle.

*Principal* as an adjective means chief or main; as a noun it means the chief person in a school, the head of the school. *Principle* is a noun meaning a basic truth or theory. A useful way to remember the difference might be to think of the *principal* as your *pal*; you can never make friends with *principles*.

### Prioritize.

It is difficult to pin down any meaning for this pompous word. If you want your reader to know clearly what you're talking about, use a more precise term. Instead of saying *If you've taken on too many obligations, prioritize your tasks*, say *do the most important ones first*.

### Prior to.

This sounds impressive, but the simple word *before* is more likely to impress the right people.

### Quality.

Quality is a noun; don't use it as an adjective. Don't speak, that is, of a *quality athlete*, despite the way sports reporters speak. This phrase sounds good but means almost nothing.

### Reason is because, reason why.

These expressions are redundant. All reasons give the *cause* or tell *why*. Say rather *the reason is that* . . . . *The reason I crashed the car is because the brakes failed* or worse, *the reason why I crashed the car is because the brakes failed* can be replaced by *the reason I crashed the car is that the brakes failed* or, better yet, *I crashed the car because the brakes failed*.

### Regard, reguard.

*Regard* does not come from *guard*; therefore, *reguard* is wrong unless, of course, you mean *guard again*.

### Round.

See *unique*.

### Separate, seperate.

Although *seperate* may sound like the correct spelling, it isn't. Think of an *ax* splitting wood, sep*a*rating one bit from another. *A* for *ax*, *a* for *separate*.

### Should of.

See *could of, should of, would of*.

### Situation.

A pompous word, often used just for padding. *Emergency situation* sounds important, but *emergency* gets the point across more effectively.

### So, such.

*So* and *such* require a clause to express result: *He was so big that he couldn't fit in the back seat. The car was painted such an ugly colour that I drove it off a cliff.*

In colloquial usage, these words often appear without the result clause (*The movie was so interesting! I had such a good time!*), but this usage is inappropriate for college writing.

### Square.

See *unique*.

### State-of-the-art.

A technical phrase referring to current technological achievements. When used in a more general sense, it is jargon and should be avoided.

### Subsequent.

Pompous for *after*, *later*, or *next*.

### Such as.

A list introduced by *such as* is, by definition, only a selection. Therefore it is inappropriate to add *etc.* at the end of the list, for that tells the reader that the list goes on and on. Thus, avoid a sentence like this: *He eats healthful food such as oats, bran, nuts, etc.* Remember too that you need no punctuation after *such as*—no comma, no colon. (See pp. 45–6.)

### Supposed, used.

Because these words are almost always followed by *to*, many people do not hear the final *d* and omit it in writing. *He is supposed to do it; I am not used to doing it.*

### Swam, swum.

*Swam* is the past tense of *swim*, *swum* the past participle. *I swam five laps yesterday but have swum only three today.*

### That.

Avoid constructions such as *that bed-time feeling*. This is the way advertizers talk. Students write essays, not commercials. (See p. 92.)

### "The".

Using quotation marks to emphasize a word, especially a minor word like *the* (*Football is "the" sport for excitement*) is another device of advertizers and thus inappropriate for college writing.

### The fact that.

Often a wordy and indirect expression. *The fact that she was the boss's daughter meant that she got the job.* See if you can find a more concise expression. *Because she was . . . she got the job.*

### Themselves, themself.

There is no such word as *themself*. It appears sometimes as a mistake in sentences where the writer does not want to commit the pronoun to a specific gender. (*Everyone enjoyed themself.*) The writer recognizes that the pronoun should be singular by using -*self*; *them*, however, should be singular too. Say *Everyone enjoyed himself* or *They all enjoyed themselves* or *We enjoyed ourselves*. (See p. 79.)

**Then, than.**

*Then* means at that time. *Than* is used in comparisons. *Then she said she liked taxis better than buses.*

**There, their, they're.**

Remember that *there* is the opposite of *here* but has the same ending. This form is used in such constructions as *There are three oranges in the box*. *Their* means belonging to them. *Their wedding cost $5,000*. *They're*, like *it's* and *who's*, is a contraction; it is short for *they are*. Until you thoroughly know the difference between these words, catch yourself every time you use one of them, and, referring to this page, make sure you're using the right word.

**This kind, this sort, this type.**

*Kind, sort*, and *type* are singular and must take singular modifiers. Thus, *I like this kind of car*, not *I like those kind of car* (or *cars*). (See pp. 96–7.) Remember too that *kind of a, sort of a, type of a* are wrong; omit *a*. Not *What kind of an animal are you?* but *What kind of animal are you?*

**Through, thru.**

*Thru* is not a word. You may see it on roadsigns (*thruway*) because drivers have only a few seconds to take in the sign and need shortened words. People often use *thru* as a kind of abbreviation (*Mondays thru Fridays*)—fair enough for informal notes, but inappropriate for anything more formal.

**To.**

Don't use *to* where you should use *or* in approximating numbers, but if you do use it, be sure to show that you are describing an interval *from* one number *to* another. Thus, *He recovered three to four months later* should be changed to *He recovered three or four months later* or *It took him from three to four months to recover*.

**Too.**

Remember that *too* has two meanings: it means also (*I want to come too*), and it means in excess (*He ate too many chocolates*). Make sure you don't use *to* when you should be using *too*.

**Try and, try to.**

Don't substitute *try and* for *try to*. You do not *try and do* a job as though you were performing two separate activities; you *try*, you make the effort, *to do* the job.

### Uninterested.

See *disinterested, uninterested.*

### Unique, perfect, square, round, dead, complete, pregnant.

These words are called "absolutes" and cannot be qualified. Something is either *unique* (one of a kind) or it's not; it cannot be *very unique*, just as something cannot be *rather square, somewhat round, less perfect, extremely dead, more complete*, and a woman cannot be *very pregnant*. (See p. 92.) The "more perfect union" spoken of in the Constitution is an exception to the rule.

### Used.

See *supposed, used.*

### Well.

See *good, well.*

### Whether, weather.

Don't confuse these two words. *Whether* indicates a choice (*She didn't know whether to go or not*); *weather* refers to the atmospheric conditions.

### Who, whom.

It is grammatically correct to say "Whom do you wish to see?" but you can safely use *who* at the beginning of a sentence as by far the more natural way of writing. Note: Few things look more silly than a writer using *whom* where it does not belong in an attempt to sound impressively correct. (See pp. 81–2.)

### Whose, who's.

*Whose* is a possessive pronoun meaning *of whom*; *who's* is a contraction of *who is. The doctor asked, "Who's the one whose throat hurts?"*

### Would of.

See *could of, should of, would of.*

# Forbidden Word List

1. Avoid these non-specific words that often produce dull and inexact writing. Instead, use other, dynamic words that can add vigor to your writing by imparting concrete images to the reader.

| | | | |
|---|---|---|---|
| awful | fine | great | stuff |
| bad | fun | interesting | sure |
| beautiful | funny | lovely | terrible |
| big | good | nice | thing |
| enjoyable | gorgeous | pretty | ugly |
| exciting | grand | real | wonderful |

2. Avoid these words because they are over-emphatic. Too often they can distort your meaning because they are too strong for the meaning you might intend.

| | | | |
|---|---|---|---|
| amazing | fabulous | perfect | terrific |
| ancient | marvelous | splendid | tremendous |
| awesome | outstanding | super | unique |
| bizarre | | | |

3. Avoid the following "Tarzan and Jane" verbs. You can easily replace them with more vivid verbs.

| | | | |
|---|---|---|---|
| come | give | make | see |
| do | go | put | talk |
| get | jump | run | walk |

AND

forms of the verb *to be*: am, are, is, were, been

4. Avoid these intensifiers, which have been so overused that they no longer carry any meaning.

| | |
|---|---|
| actually | certainly |
| awfully | personally |
| basically | really |

# Irregular Verb List

The following are the most commonly used irregular verbs. When in doubt about which form to use, consult this list or look in the dictionary, which will give the principal parts of all irregular verbs.

| PRESENT | PAST | PAST PARTICIPLE |
| --- | --- | --- |
| arise | arose | arisen |
| awake | awoke/awakened | awoken/awakened |
| be (am, are, is) | was (were) | been |
| bear | bore | born/borne |
| beat | beat | beaten |
| become | became | become |
| begin | began | begun |
| bend | bent | bent |
| bet | bet | bet |
| bite | bit | bitten |
| blow | blew | blown |
| break | broke | broken |
| bring | brought | brought |
| build | built | built |
| burst | burst | burst |

N.B. There is no such verb in standard English as *bust*.

APPENDIX C

| PRESENT | PAST | PAST PARTICIPLE |
| --- | --- | --- |
| buy | bought | bought |
| catch | caught | caught |
| choose | chose | chosen |
| come | came | come |
| cost | cost | cost |
| cut | cut | cut |
| dive | dived/dove | dived |
| do (does) | did | done |
| draw | drew | drawn |
| drink | drank | drunk |

N.B. The noun is *drunk*; the adjective is *drunken*.

| PRESENT | PAST | PAST PARTICIPLE |
| --- | --- | --- |
| drive | drove | driven |
| eat | ate | eaten |
| fall | fell | fallen |
| feed | fed | fed |
| feel | felt | felt |
| fight | fought | fought |
| find | found | found |
| fly | flew | flown |
| forbid | forbade/forbad | forbidden |
| forget | forgot | forgot/forgotten |
| forgive | forgave | forgiven |
| freeze | froze | frozen |
| get | got | got/gotten |
| give | gave | given |
| go (goes) | went | gone |
| grow | grew | grown |
| have (has) | had | had |
| hear | heard | heard |
| hide | hid | hidden |
| hit | hit | hit |
| hold | held | held |
| hurt | hurt | hurt |
| keep | kept | kept |
| know | knew | known |
| lay | laid | laid |
| lead | led | led |
| leave | left | left |
| lend | lent | lent |
| let | let | let |
| lie | lay | lain |
| light | lit | lit |
| lose | lost | lost |
| make | made | made |
| mean | meant | meant |
| meet | met | met |
| pay | paid | paid |

IRREGULAR VERB LIST

| PRESENT | PAST | PAST PARTICIPLE |
|---------|------|-----------------|
| read | read | read |
| ride | rode | ridden |
| ring | rang | rung |
| rise | rose | risen |
| run | ran | run |
| say | said | said |
| see | saw | seen |
| sell | sold | sold |
| send | sent | sent |
| shake | shook | shaken |
| shine | shone | shone |
| shrink | shrank | shrunk |
| shut | shut | shut |
| sing | sang | sung |
| sink | sank/sunk | sunk |

N.B. *Sunken* is an adjective.

| PRESENT | PAST | PAST PARTICIPLE |
|---------|------|-----------------|
| sit | sat | sat |
| sleep | slept | slept |
| speak | spoke | spoken |
| spend | spent | spent |
| spin | span | spun |
| spring | sprang/sprung | sprung |
| stand | stood | stood |
| steal | stole | stolen |
| stick | stuck | stuck |
| swear | swore | sworn |
| swim | swam | swum |
| swing | swung | swung |
| take | took | taken |
| tear | tore | torn |
| throw | threw | thrown |
| wear | wore | worn |
| weave | wove/weaved | woven/weaved |
| weep | wept | wept |
| win | won | won |
| wind | wound | wound |
| wring | wrung | wrung |
| write | wrote | written |

# Commonly Misspelled Words

The words on the following list have given many people trouble. The problem area of each word is indicated.

| | | | |
|---|---|---|---|
| aba*ndon*ed | bene*fic*ial | co*n*ce*n*trate | destroy |
| ac*c*eptable | benefit | confu*se* | destruction |
| ach*ie*ve | bu*si*ness | confu*s*ion | di*ff*erence |
| a*l*cohol | | conve*ni*ence | di*ff*erent |
| all right | ca*reer* | conve*ni*ent | di*ni*ng |
| alth*ough* | cha*lle*nge | cred*it* | di*scrim*inate |
| analyze | chance | crim*in*al | di*scrim*ination |
| ar*thr*itis | chan*g*e | crow*d*ed | di*s*cuss |
| as*s*ist | cho*ice* | cu*s*tom | drow*ned* |
| as*s*istance | choose | | drow*ni*ng |
| a*thl*ete | chosen | deceive | d*ue* |
| a*thl*etic | co*m*fortable | deception | |
| | co*mmerc*ial | decision | *ei*ther |
| beca*use* | co*mm*it | define | emba*rra*ss |
| begin*n*ing | competit*i*on | definite | enforce |
| bel*ief*(s) | co*m*plain | defin*it*ely | en*ough* |
| bel*ie*vable | co*m*plain*t* | describe | enro*ll*ment |
| bel*ie*ve | conce*i*ted | description | envi*ron*ment |

APPENDIX D

except
exception
exceptional
excite
expect
expectation
experience
explain
explanation
extremely

feeling
finances
financial
fortunate
fortunately
forward
fulfil
fulfilment
future

govern
government
governor
grateful

handicap
handicapped
heroin
hospital

immediate
important
independence
independent
individual
instance
institution

interest
interesting
interpret
involve
involvement

jealous
jealously

know
knowledge

listen
listener

medical
medicine
messenger
mind
mine
mugged
murder
murderer

necessary
necessity
negative
nowadays

occasion
occur
opinion
opportunity

patience
patient
physical
physically

possess
possession
possibility
possible
pregnancy
pregnant
privilege
privileged
probability
probable
probably
problem
professional
proof
prove

quiet
quite

react
reaction
really
receive
reception
recognize
register
registration
rehabilitate
relief
relieve
repeat
repetitious
responsibility
responsible
restaurant
restrict
restriction
ridiculous

robbed
robber

sale
satisfaction
satisfied
sell
separate
similar
statistics
strict
succeed
success
support
surprise
survive

temporary
tendency
than
their
themselves
then
there
through
truly

usual

violence
violent

weigh
where
whether

yield

# How to
# use the
# Dictionary

As a college student, you are expected to know how to use a dictionary. Dictionaries, however, often turn out to be more complicated and more confusing than you may have anticipated, and it is worth spending a few minutes understanding what a dictionary has to offer so you can proceed with confidence.

There are three categories of dictionaries—unabridged, collegiate and pocket. The unabridged dictionaries contain comprehensive entries on all words in English. They are too large and expensive for most people to buy, but most good libraries will have at least one unabridged dictionary available for reference. You wouldn't want to use these dictionaries just to look up the spelling of a word; they are most useful for providing comprehensive definitions of words and illustrating through examples acceptable ways to use words in sentences.

Collegiate dictionaries are usually shortened versions of the unabridged dictionaries. These are the dictionaries to buy and keep by your side the rest of your career. These dictionaries give full definitions to more than 150,000 words, indicate the origin of the words (their etymology), differentiate between synonyms, and provide guidelines to word usage by labelling some words as slang, non-standard, technical, etc. Some recommended college dictionaries are *Webster's New Collegiate Dictionary*, *Webster's New World*

APPENDIX E

*Dictionary, The American Heritage Dictionary* (College Edition), and the *Random House Dictionary* (College Edition).

The third kind of dictionary is the small, often paperback, pocket dictionary. These dictionaries are, of course, cheaper than the other two, and, if you are simply going to look up an ordinary word's spelling, they are adequate for the job. The trouble comes when you require more complicated information. The definitions are scanty, often just one word, and there is no indication of how to use the word. Because these dictionaries contain many fewer entries than the other two kinds, you may look in vain for obscure or technical words or for alternative forms of words. If you're using a pocket dictionary, know its limitations and don't hesitate to turn to a larger one for more complex problems.

# • How the dictionary works

The best way to learn what a dictionary is all about is to read the guide to the dictionary found near the beginning of the book. Because each major dictionary differs in some respects from the others, it is important to learn your dictionary's policies and the way it is organized. To give you an idea of how one commonly used dictionary works, let us run through the entry for *remember* in *Webster's Ninth New Collegiate Dictionary.* You can check the corresponding entry in your own dictionary for possible variations in approach.

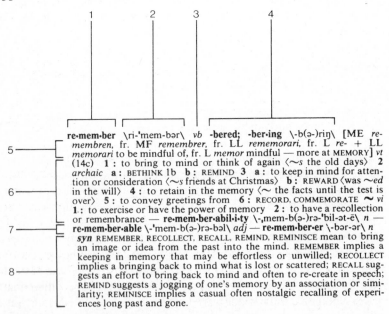

By permission. From *Webster's Ninth New Collegiate Dictionary* © 1987 by Merriam-Webster Inc., publisher of the Merriam-Webster ® dictionaries.

HOW TO USE THE DICTIONARY

1. *Spelling and syllabication.* The entry begins with the word itself printed in boldface (darker and thicker type), and this gives us the accepted spelling and indicates with a raised dot where the word breaks into syllables: *re·mem·ber.* When you find two spellings of a word joined by *or* ("ax *or* axe"), you may choose either spelling. If the two spellings, however, are joined by *also* ("camellia *also* camelia"), regard the first as the preferred spelling. This part of the entry will also tell you whether to hyphenate a compound word (*battle-ax*), leave it as two words (*battle cruiser*), or write it as one word (*bat·tle·field*). Dictionaries may vary about how to treat the same word, but as long as you can cite a relatively recent, respectable American dictionary to support your usage, you should face no trouble. (Check first, though, to see if your organization or your teacher prefers one dictionary over another.)

2. *Pronunciation.* Following the boldface entry, the pronunciation of the word is indicated, set off by diagonal lines. At the bottom of the page you will find an explanation of the symbols used to indicate pronunciation. The raised vertical line before *mem* ('*mem*) indicates that the second syllable is accented. (In other dictionaries, the accent mark may come *after* the stressed syllable.) In longer words, both a major and a minor stress may be indicated (ˌdem·on·'stra·tion). More than one pronunciation may be listed; if there is no indication that one is a preferred pronunciation, use whichever sounds the most familiar.

3. *Part of Speech.* *Vb* tells us that *remember* is a verb. Note: Part-of-speech labels and other abbreviations are explained in the opening guidelines to the dictionary.

4. *Inflectional forms.* The dictionary will list the past, past participle, and present participle forms of irregular verbs or the plurals of nouns if they are formed other than simply by adding *s*. In our example, the forms of the past tense and the present participle are given because their pronunciation varies. The (ə-) indicates that some speakers do not pronounce the third *e* in *remembered* or *remembering*.

5. *Etymology.* Although for ordinary occasions most readers and writers do not need to know where a word came from, it can be helpful to know the way a word has developed since that sometimes may indicate certain nuances in its meaning. The etymological explanation for our entry (enclosed in brackets) tells us that *remember* comes from the Middle English word *rememberen*, which comes from the Middle French *remembrer*, which in turn comes from the Late Latin form *rememorari*, formed from the Latin *re-* and *memorari*, meaning "to be mindful of," which in its turn comes from *memor*, "mindful." For further derivations, we are advised to look up the word *memory*.

6. *The definition.* The definition of *remember* is in two parts, first for the verb when transitive (*vt*), second when intransitive (*vi*). (For the

APPENDIX E

distinction between transitive and intransitive verbs, see pp. 13–4.) The parenthetical note before the first definition tells us the date of the earliest recorded use of the word in English; (*14c*) indicates that *remember* first appeared in English in the fourteenth century. The six senses of the transitive and the two of the intransitive form are listed in the order in which they first began to be used in English. Thus *remember* meant "to bring to mind" before it meant, say, "to retain in the mind." (Note: Many dictionaries list the most frequently used sense of the word first. Knowing the order can be crucial if you are looking up a completely unknown word. Once again, consult the opening guide to the dictionary to learn how your dictionary arranges the definition.)

The italicized word *archaic* in the second meaning is a *usage label* and indicates that since the mid-eighteenth century, the word has been used in this sense only in special contexts. (*She remembered me of my mother.*) The words in capital letters (BETHINK, REMIND, REWARD, RECORD, COMMEMORATE) are cross references: the definitions found under these words fit the sense of the word in the present entry.

Phrases illustrating the usage of the word appear in angled brackets after many of the senses. Replace the swung dash (∼) in the illustration with the main word of the entry. Thus <∼s the old days> should be read <remembers the old days>.

7. *Run-on entry.* After the definition of the word, there may be listed one or more derivatives, or words formed from the main word, in our example, the noun *rememberability*, the adjective *rememberable*, and the noun *rememberer*. These words are followed by partial pronunciation guides to show how that third *e* is pronounced.

8. *Synonymy.* A synonymy distinguishes among several different synonyms. *Remember, recollect, recall, remind, reminisce* have similar meanings, but the synonymy explains the specific senses in which each word is generally used. In the entries for *recollect, recall, remind,* and *reminisce*, the reader is referred to this synonymy by the notice "**syn** see REMEMBER."

# • Other features of the dictionary

Don't forget the various "extras" provided by dictionaries. *Webster's Ninth*, for instance, offers

Abbreviations and symbols for chemical elements

A list of foreign words and phrases

Separate listings for biographical names and geographical names

A list of American colleges and universities (with addresses)

Signs and symbols

A handbook of style

The *Random House Dictionary* has many of these features as well as a historical sketch of the English language and a table of common English spellings. The *American Heritage Dictionary* also has articles on "English vs. good English," and the *New World Dictionary* gives a table of weights and measures and a list of forms of address.

# INDEX

INDEX

INDEX

INDEX

INDEX

| SYMBOL | PAGE NUMBERS | MEANING |
|---|---|---|
| ab | 66–67 | faulty abbreviation |
| ad | 20–25, 91–94 | faulty use of adjective or adverb |
| agr | 83–87 | faulty subject-verb agreement |
| ap | 55–57 | faulty or missing apostrophe |
| awk | 75 | awkward sentence structure |
| ca | 81–82 | wrong pronoun case |
| coh | 123–25 | weak paragraph coherence |
| com | 46–53 | faulty or missing comma |
| comp | 99–101 | faulty comparison |
| d | 119–21 | inappropriate diction |
| dev | 125–26 | weak paragraph development |
| dgl | 94–95 | dangling modifier |
| ef | 103–8 | ineffective sentence |
| emp | 112–16 | lack of emphasis |
| end p | 40–43 | mistake in end punctuation |
| frag | 72–74 | sentence fragment |
| glos | 129–42 | see glossary of usage |
| nos | 65 | error in use of numbers |
| q | 58–61 | error in punctuating quoted material |
| ref | 76–78 | error in pronoun reference |
| ro | 74–75 | run-on sentence |
| semi | 43–44 | error in use of semicolon |
| sp | 149–50 | misspelling |
| sub | 105–10 | faulty or missing subordination |
| syl | 153 | improper division of word |